Contents

Credits

PEARSON
PUBLISHING

Student Handbook for ICT: GCSE

Gareth Williams

Hands off!

This book belongs to:

Name..

Class..

School..

Date of exams ....

Coursework deadline dates ....

Exam board...

Syllabus number ....

Candidate number...

Centre number...

Further copies of this publication may be obtained from:
Pearson Publishing
Chesterton Mill, French's Road, Cambridge CB4 3NP
Tel 01223 350555   Fax 01223 356484
Email info@pearson.co.uk   Web site www.pearsonpublishing.co.uk

ISBN: 978 1 85749 874 5
Published by Pearson Publishing 2004
© Pearson Publishing 2004

First published 2003
Second edition 2003
Third edition 2005
Fourth edition 2008

Introduction

Today's world is dominated by technology and the world of computing is changing constantly. This new and exciting handbook has been designed not just to show you how technology works, but to help prepare you for living in the real world. It also gives you an idea of just how important technology is.

The handbook is designed for students in Years 10 and 11 who are studying GCSE ICT. It provides comprehensive coverage of the subject, including hardware, software, data, networks, applications of ICT and the effect ICT has on society.

Using this handbook

Each topic is presented as a short, self-contained unit, with clear pictures and illustrations. An icon ⊕ is used to guide you to other related information in the book. The contents page has been designed in the form of a checklist so that you can track your progress and an index is provided at the back of the handbook to help you to find specific topics.

Key points, which summarise the section, are included at the end of four of the main topics (ie hardware, software, data and networks). These should prove useful for revision.

Multiple-choice questions to test your knowledge are provided at the end, together with a grid in which you can record your answers. Answers to the questions are also included. In addition, some advice on answering written exam questions is also offered.

A grid linking topics to syllabuses is included at the end of the handbook.

Feedback

If you have any comments or suggestions as to how this book may be improved, please send them to the author via Pearson Publishing.

Computers are placed into groups according to their size, processing power, design and cost. These groups are:

- Supercomputers
- Mainframe computers
- Microcomputers
- Personal digital assistants (PDAs)
- Embedded computers.

Supercomputers

Supercomputers are the fastest and the most expensive computers. Thousands of processing chips work together to provide their huge processing power. The latest supercomputers are able to perform 200 000 000 000 000 (two hundred trillion) calculations per second. These computers are used for scientific and engineering applications such as forecasting the weather or performing very complex graphical techniques.

Mainframe computers

Mainframe computers are very powerful and can have hundreds of simultaneous users. They are used by large companies for data processing, by scientists for complex mathematical calculations and as network servers on the Internet.

Personal digital assistants (PDAs)

On these small hand-held computers, data is input using a stylus (pen) on a touch-sensitive screen. Built-in software recognises and converts handwriting into computer text. PDAs hold software for storing contacts information, keeping a diary, making notes, playing games and sending and receiving emails. These computers are also known as palmtop devices.

Computers in this group are the most common and include the computers we use at home, in school and in most businesses. Computers within the group can be further divided into desktop and notebook computers. The illustration on the right shows the usual features of a microcomputer.

The type and speed of the processor or central processing unit (CPU) broadly determine the power of the computer. A typical processor would be a Core 2 Duo, with two processor cores running at 2.0 GHz each (2000 million operations per second).

Case containing motherboard, with processor (CPU), RAM and hard disk

CD, DVD or combined drive

Monitor

Thin, flat TFT screen

Keyboard

Mouse

Laptop computers

Laptop computers (also known as notebooks) are light and easy to carry around. The low power, miniaturised components and the thin film transistor (TFT) screen ⑤▷ make the computer more expensive than desktops of similar power. For ultra-light and thin laptops, DVD or CD-ROM drives are connected to the computer only when needed. Some laptops can be placed into a docking station which has connections to a printer, network and power supply.

TFT screen

Touch pad

CD/DVD drive

Connections at the back

Embedded computers

From telephones to missiles, and from cameras to washing machines, many modern devices contain built-in computers or embedded systems. There is no need for these systems to use keyboards and computer monitors since the inputs required come from the device's sensors, and outputs control the operation of the device.

Keyboard

The standard keyboard illustrated below is called a QWERTY keyboard as these are the first six keys on the top row of letters. The basic layout of the keys is similar in many countries although slight variations are necessary where languages use additional letters in their alphabets. Some keyboards are designed with a curved key layout to make typing faster and more comfortable.

In comparison with other input devices, entering data using a keyboard is quite slow, even for touch-typists who have learnt to type using all their fingers and thumbs without needing to look at the keyboard.

Braille keyboards

People who are visually impaired use Braille code. This consists of letters and symbols that are read by fingers moving across a series of raised dots. To enter data, Braille notetakers can be plugged directly into a computer or tactile (touch) overlays can be placed over certain keys on the QWERTY keyboard.

Concept keyboard

A concept keyboard consists of a flat panel of contact switches covered by a flexible membrane. Each switch can be programmed to respond in different ways by the computer software. Overlays with pictures and symbols are placed over the membrane. These keyboards are popular in primary schools where young children can just press on the symbols and pictures on the overlay. Concept keyboards are also used in restaurants where the checkout tills use symbols to speed up data entry. They can also be found in hostile environments. For example, on oil rigs where the membrane protects the keyboard from being damaged by salt spray and chemicals.

Trackerball

A trackerball is similar to a mouse but the ball is set into a cup on the top of the unit. A finger or, on larger trackerballs, the palm of the hand, is used to roll the ball in any direction. The ball controls the movement of the pointer on the screen. Buttons on the trackerball work in the same way as mouse buttons to activate processes on the screen.

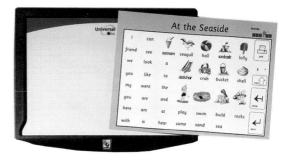

Mouse

The movement of the mouse by the user's hand is mirrored by the pointer on the monitor screen. Some mice still have a ball underneath them  which moves as the mouse is moved, but most mice are **optical**, and use a light beam and detector instead. The mouse shines a beam of light at the surface it is on, and movement is detected via changes in the way the light is reflected back off the surface. When the screen pointer is over an icon or menu selection, the mouse button can be clicked, double-clicked or dragged (moved with the button held down) to activate a process.

Most mice have a small wheel as well as the buttons. The function of the wheel depends on the software being used on the computer: in a document, it can allow the user to scroll up and down; in a desktop publishing package, it might enable the user to zoom in and out of the page.

Many mice now use infra-red or wireless links to the computer so no connecting cable is necessary.

Graphics tablet

The graphics tablet is a flat pad which the user can write or draw on with a device similar to a pen called a stylus. The surface of the pad is sensitive to the position of the stylus and the stylus itself is sensitive to the pressure applied by the user. As the stylus is moved across the pad, the movement is translated to a drawing on the computer monitor. The harder the user presses on the stylus, the thicker the line drawn on the screen. A typical resolution for a graphics tablet used in art work and computer aided design (CAD) is $1/1000$ cm.

Joystick

Joysticks are popular input devices for computer games. The hand grip can be moved around the central axis in any direction but is spring-loaded to return to the centre when the hand pressure is released. Joysticks have many more buttons to control the software functions. For example, when using a joystick to control a flight simulator, the buttons control the flaps, views from the cockpit, landing gear and engine speed. Some joysticks have 'force feedback' which enables the user to feel some of the forces that might be experienced in real life.

Touch pad

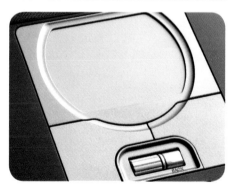

These input devices are found on laptop computers and offer the same functions as a mouse. Moving your finger across the pad controls the movement of the pointer on the screen. Tapping lightly on the pad with the finger has the same function as clicking the mouse button but switches are positioned next to the pad as well to represent the left and right mouse buttons.

Scanner

Scanners are used to input pictures and text into a computer. Scanning text in order to recognise the words and letters requires special software (this is covered below under OCR). The most common type of scanner is the flat-bed, but smaller hand-held scanners that are rolled over the document or picture are also available.

The flat-bed scanner works by placing the picture to be scanned face down on a glass plate like a photocopier. A bright light is slowly moved across the picture and the reflected light is focused onto a light-sensitive device using several mirrors and a lens. White parts of the picture reflect the most light, black parts reflect the least and colours reflect different wavelengths of light. For each tiny part of the picture, the intensity and nature of the light is captured and converted into a digital signal for input to the computer. Scanned pictures, which can be manipulated using sophisticated image editing software, are often used in publishing work.

Optical mark reader (OMR)

Optical mark readers detect marks made on paper. It is usually recommended that the marks are made with a soft (HB) pencil or a black pen. The reader scans across the paper with an infra-red light. Where there is no mark, there is a strong reflection of light off the white paper; where a mark has been made, the light reflection is reduced and this is input to the computer.

Optical mark readers are used for inputting the numbers on lottery tickets and can also be used for recording the answers on multiple-choice examination papers, for school registers and for recording gas and electricity meter readings.

Touch screen

On touch-sensitive screens there are criss-crossing beams of infra-red light in front of the glass on the monitor. When a user touches the glass with their finger, two sets of rays are blocked: the rays travelling from side to side and the rays going from top to bottom. The computer detects the finger's position from the light sensors placed on the opposite side of the monitor screen to the light sources. Touch screens are user-friendly and are used as input devices for information systems in public places like museums.

Optical character recognition (OCR)

Scanning devices using OCR software are used to recognise letters, numbers and words. The ability to scan the characters accurately depends on how clear the writing is. The software has improved to be able to read different styles and sizes of type and also neat handwriting.

One application of optical character recognition is reading postcodes on letters at sorting offices so that letters can be sorted automatically.

Light pen

A light pen is a pen-shaped device connected to the computer with a cable. It does not emit light but has a light detector in the tip of the pen that picks up the light signals from the monitor. The pen can be made to work like a mouse, selecting menus, activating programs and drawing lines on the screen. It is not a common input device but is used in art and design work.

Bar code reader

Bar codes are made up of black and white stripes of different thicknesses. These lines represent numbers and are read with a wand or laser scanner. They are now used on most goods, and provide a fast and reliable method of entering data even when the surfaces being read are curved or upside-down. The bar code numbers hold coded information about the product, including the country of manufacture, the name of the manufacturer, a product item code and a check digit. They do not hold information directly for the name, description or price of the product. When the numbers on the bar code are scanned, the data is passed to the computer which then returns information about the product.

Digital camera

The picture taken with a digital camera is stored in computer memory rather than on film as in a traditional camera. The different colours that make up the picture are converted to digital signals (codes of 0s and 1s) by sensors placed behind the lens. The pictures can be:

- displayed on the computer monitor
- imported into a graphics/art program for editing
- printed (best done using a high-quality photographic paper).

The quality of the picture is determined by the resolution of the camera and is measured in pixels ⑤. High-quality digital cameras may have a resolution of ten or more megapixels. Many cameras have their own small LCD ⑤ screen which displays the picture taken with the camera. This gives the user the option to view the picture and discard it if it is not suitable. The cost of taking pictures with a digital camera is much less than a traditional camera where a film and processing have to be purchased. An ink-jet printer ⑥ and high-quality paper are all that is required for printing digital pictures.

Web cam

A Web cam is a digital camera that sits on or by a computer. Digital images are input directly to the computer and can be used for video conferencing with other users over the network. Compared to the more expensive digital cameras, Web cam images tend to be of lower resolution and poorer quality.

Video capture

Digital camcorders can plug straight into computers through a Firewire connection, which is a very fast data link to the computer. This allows the computer to download, store and manipulate the digital video images. Older analogue ㉒ camcorders can also connect to a computer but require a video digitiser card fitted in the computer. Video capture and editing requires large amounts of computer memory so computers need to have large hard disk drives to hold these files. Special software, however, can compress files to $1/100$th of their original size with little loss in image quality.

Magnetic ink character recognition (MICR)

This method of inputting data into a computer is used on bank cheques. The important data on a bank cheque that is required when it is processed is printed along the bottom edge of the cheque as strange-looking characters. The ink used to form these characters contains tiny magnetic particles. This enables the data from each cheque to be read into the computer by machine. MICR is a fast and reliable method of reading data into a computer as it is unaffected by scribbling over the characters with a pen.

Microphone (speech or voice)

Speech or voice input is a rapidly developing means of input to a computer. It is already an important method for people who are severely handicapped, or where the user's hands need to be free to do other things, but its use is still mainly restricted to these areas.

Programs are available which recognise continuous speech input, translating the words directly into a word processor. Some words sound the same but are used in different contexts, eg 'weather' and 'whether' or 'sail' and 'sale'. These programs can select the appropriate spelling from the sentence that is spoken.

Magnetic stripe

Magnetic stripes are thin strips of magnetic tape found on the back of many types of plastic card, for example on debit and credit cards, library cards, and on cinema and train tickets. When the card is used in the reader, the stripe passes playback heads, similar to a tape recorder, which reads data from the stripe.

Cards with stripes are used, for example, to keep track of supermarket loyalty schemes.

Magnetic stripe

Smart card

A smart card (also known as an integrated chip card, or ICC) is a plastic card which contains a tiny microprocessor chip. This enables more data to be stored on the card and also enables the personal identification number (PIN) entered by the user to be checked against the information held in the chip. The data on smart cards is more secure than on cards with magnetic stripes and they have been widely adopted by banks through the 'Chip and PIN' system. Smart cards are also used for mobile phones and satellite television receivers.

Chip contact

Musical instrument digital interface (MIDI)

MIDI was developed as a standard for linking musical keyboards and instruments together. Computers fitted with MIDI interface boards can be connected to MIDI instruments allowing music to be input to and output from the computer. Software on the computer enables the music to be stored, displayed on the monitor as a musical score and edited by adding, deleting and moving notes. Music from different instruments can be added as new tracks so that one musician can create the effect of a whole orchestra.

A laptop computer linked to MIDI instruments and a digital mixer

Input devices used for control and data logging

When computers are used to collect data from the environment or to control machines then a different type of input device is needed. These are often mechanical and electronic components. Take, for example, an automated weather station.

Input devices are needed to measure temperatures, light levels, rain fall, air pressure, humidity, wind direction and strength. Several of the more common input devices are:

- **Switches** – Moving equipment or an operator can activate a push button, slide or toggle switch. Proximity switches are activated when a magnet comes close to the switch. The two contacts that form the switch make contact when in the magnetic field. Tilt switches operate as the device is raised and lowered. Tilt switches can be gas-filled sealed units or mercury switches where a bead of mercury runs along inside the tube forming a contact.

- **Thermistors** – Thermistors are used to measure temperature. Their electrical resistance decreases as the temperature rises. This change is converted into a digital input signal to the computer.

- **Light-dependent resistors (LDRs)** – Light-dependent resistors are light sensors that change their electrical resistance according to the amount of light falling on them. The brighter the light, the lower the resistance. These, together with heat sensors, could be used in a computer automated greenhouse to maintain the ideal growing conditions for the plants.

Automated weather station

The monitor, screen or VDU (visual display unit) is the most common computer output device. Popular screen sizes are 15 inches (38 cm) and 17 inches (43 cm). The size is always measured diagonally, from corner to corner, but beware – the size of the screen you see is less than the quoted size as some of the screen is hidden behind the plastic rim of the monitor casing. The screen sizes for televisions are also measured in this way. Larger monitors make working at a computer easier on the eyes and are essential for use in desktop publishing and design work.

Traditional monitors

Traditional computer monitors are similar to televisions in using a cathode ray tube (CRT). On the back of the glass screen is a coating of small phosphor dots that glow when hit by the beam of electrons coming from the back of the tube. The phosphor dots are arranged in groups of three; one red, one green and one blue dot. By hitting the colours with beams of different intensities, a wide range of colours is produced. The three dots are so close together that the human eye sees them as just one colour.

Groups of dots are called **pixels** (short for picture elements). The more pixels there are on the screen, the clearer and sharper the image. The clarity of the picture is measured by its **resolution**. The more pixels a screen has, the higher its resolution. Three standards in current use are:

- SVGA (super video graphics array) – 800 x 600 pixels
- XGA (extended graphics array) – 1024 x 768 pixels
- SXGA (super extended graphics array) – 1280 x 1024 pixels

Screens of the future

The hunt is on for a new display technology that will combine the portability of LCD with the cheapness and simplicity of CRT, while going further than either in terms of performance and adaptability. Competing developments include flat screens using light-emitting polymers (LEPs) and forms of so-called 'electronic paper'.

Liquid crystal displays (LCDs)

Liquid crystal displays utilise tiny crystals which, when a charge is applied across them, polarise the light passing through them. Used in combination with special filters, this means that light will not pass through when an electrical charge is applied. LCDs are also used in watches and calculators.

Laptop screens and flat panel monitors

Laptops and flat panel monitors use thin film transistor (TFT) screens. In this specialised form of LCD, each screen pixel is controlled by its own transistor and the active matrix gives full colour and high resolution images. Although TFT screens are slightly more expensive than traditional CRT monitors, they take up much less desk space and are much lighter thus making them a popular choice in homes, schools and businesses.

Projectors

A digital projector connects directly into the back of the computer and projects a bright, sharp image on the screen. In recent years, the price of projectors has fallen, while the portability, bulb life and image brightness have all increased. Projectors are used in business for training and presentations and in education for lessons and lectures. Key features include:

- **Brightness** – The brightness of the image determines how large the screen can be and whether the unit can be used in a room with normal lighting conditions, eg a classroom. Early projectors were only effective in rooms with near blackout conditions. Brightness is measured in lumens; a typical school projector has a brightness of 1800 lumens.
- **Bulb life** – Projector bulbs are expensive and have a bulb life of 2000 hours.
- **Mounting** – Projectors are quite light (ie 2 to 4 kg) and can be carried between rooms and set up on a stand or table. Permanent fixings are often mounted in the ceiling.
- **Remote control** – When a projector is used, an infra-red device or laser pointer is often used in place of a mouse.
- **Cost** – Between £400 and £1000.

Traditionally, printers have been divided into two groups: **impact** and **non-impact**. Impact printers involve mechanisms where the characters are formed by striking the paper through an inked ribbon. Because of this hammering, impact printers can be quite noisy when printing. Dot-matrix printers are impact printers. Laser and ink-jet printers are non-impact printers.

Dot-matrix printer

A dot-matrix printer has a printhead which travels across the paper. In the head is a set of pins that shoot out and strike the ink ribbon against the paper as the printhead moves along. These printers produce low- to medium-quality black and white printing. Several years ago they were the ideal choice for a home printer but now the colour ink-jet has taken their place. They are still used in business for the following reasons:

- The running costs are very low.
- They are robust and can operate in harsh environments.

- If several sheets of self-carbonating paper are placed into the printer, then multiple copies can be produced at the same time. This is because it is an impact printer and strikes the paper. This is particularly useful in places such as warehouses.

Plotters

There are several types of plotter. The flat-bed plotter, commonly found in school design and technology departments, uses precision motors controlled by the computer. These motors move an arm across the paper in the 'x' direction and the pen unit up and down the arm in the 'y' direction. An electromagnet lifts and drops the pen onto the paper.

Plotters are often used in science and engineering applications for drawing building plans, printed circuit boards, machines and machine parts. They are accurate to hundredths of a millimetre and can be the size of a small classroom! However, the increase in the quality of low-priced A2 and A3 size colour ink-jet printers has reduced the demand for smaller plotters.

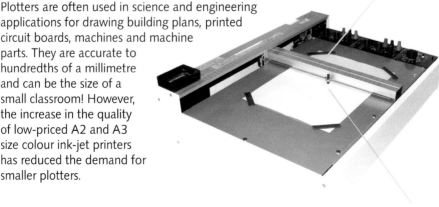

Mechanical arm

Pen

Ink-jet printer

In an ink-jet printer, the printhead contains tiny nozzles through which ink can be selectively sprayed onto the paper to form the characters or the graphic images. Inside the printhead are tiny piezoelectric crystals. These crystals change shape when an electric current is applied across them and this forces the ink out through the printhead nozzle.

The bubble-jet printer is a type of ink-jet printer but instead of the ink being forced out of the printhead, it is heated rapidly. This causes the ink to boil and a bubble of ink is formed. As the bubble forms, it expands and is forced through the nozzle of the printhead and onto the paper.

Ink-jet and bubble-jet printers are relatively inexpensive and produce high-quality black and white or colour printing. This makes them a popular choice for home and school use. The printing speed is slower than a laser printer but for small quantities of printing it is more economical, particularly for colour printing.

Laser printer

Laser printers are popular in businesses and in schools. They are fast and quiet and for large quantities of printing they can be very economical.

The laser draws the image of the page onto a negatively-charged photosensitive drum. Where the laser hits the drum, the charge is removed. The drum then passes a toner reservoir where negatively-charged toner (powdered ink) is attracted to the areas where the charge has been removed. This toner is transferred to the paper as it passes the drum. The toner is then melted onto the paper by the pressure and heat of the fuser unit, producing the final printed copy. Colour laser printers use four toner units – one with black ink and three with coloured inks – that combine to form high-quality, full colour prints.

Mono (black) printers can be purchased for less than £50 and colour laser printers for around £200. More expensive printers have larger paper trays and faster printing speeds. They offer double-sided printing and even hard disk drives to store documents.

The speed of a laser printer is measured in pages per minute (ppm). A typical mono printer would have a speed of 16 ppm.

Speakers for sound and voice output

Computers can output both music and speech to speakers or headphones. Synthesised speech output, generated from a computer program, can be particularly useful for blind users where passages of text or figures from a spreadsheet are spoken.

One common example of speech synthesis is used by directory enquiry services. When you call them, the operator searches a computer database and locates the number you need. A computer then reads this number out to you by saying, "The number you require is...".

Control applications

When computers are used to control the movement of mechanisms and machines, the output devices are switches and actuators.

Switches

Output signals from a computer are of low voltage and power. For these tiny pulses of electricity to control machines, the signals are boosted using electronic components, for example, silicon controlled rectifiers (SCR). Switches can turn electrical equipment 'on' or 'off' and can operate solenoid valves (see the illustration below) to control the flow of air and fluids through pipes.

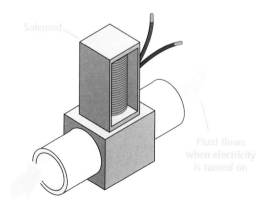

A control signal from the computer switches the electricity on. The electricity flowing through the coil produces an electromagnet which lifts a valve in the pipe allowing the fluid to flow

Light-emitting diodes (LEDs)

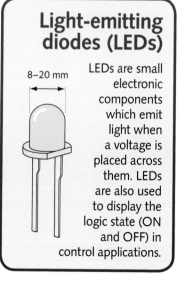

8–20 mm

LEDs are small electronic components which emit light when a voltage is placed across them. LEDs are also used to display the logic state (ON and OFF) in control applications.

Actuators

Signals from computers can generate physical movement in certain control devices. These devices are called actuators and include motors, hydraulics and pneumatics.

Motors

There are two types of electrical motor. The first is the 'ordinary' electrical motor which turns continuously while the power is on. For example, the motor that drives the drum on a washing machine. The second type is the stepper motor where each electrical pulse from the computer rotates the motor shaft by a tiny amount. For a typical motor this might be a turn of 1.8°, hence 200 pulses would be needed to turn the shaft of the motor through one complete revolution. Stepper motors give very precise movements and are used in printers, plotters and robotic arms.

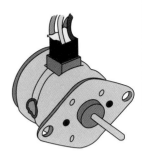

Stepper motor

Hydraulics

Here the output from the computer controls the movement of hydraulic rams by pumping oil. These hydraulic rams, similar to those seen on mechanical diggers and bulldozers, can be slow but are very powerful.

Pneumatics

Pneumatics are quite similar to hydraulics in using rams but the pistons are powered by air rather than oil. Pneumatics are not as powerful as the hydraulic systems but the movement of the rams is much faster.

Computers can control the movement of rams. These can be operated by air (pneumatics) or oil (hydraulics)

A robot arm can be controlled by motors, hydraulics or pneumatics. The type of system used depends on the application, ie:

- most accurate movement – motors
- fastest movement – pneumatics
- most powerful – hydraulics.

When operating, all computers use computer programs and data. The storage devices that are used to hold these, even when the computer is switched off, are described in this section.

Hard disks

Hard disks are a common form of data storage on most computers, both on stand-alone and networked computers. A typical microcomputer purchased for home or school may have a disk capacity of 120 gigabytes. This would hold the operating system (eg Microsoft® Windows), applications (word processor, spreadsheet, database, etc), games and the data from programs. On larger systems, the hard disks may hold terabytes (1024 GB) of storage.

Disk platters, where the data is stored

Rotating arm

Read/write heads

Data is stored by magnetising the surface of a flat, circular plate. These plates rotate at high speed, typically 60 to 120 revolutions per second. A read/write head floats on a cushion of air a fraction of a millimetre above the surface of the disk. It is so close that even a smoke particle on the disk would cause the heads to crash. For this reason, the drive is inside a sealed unit.

External drives

As the price of hard discs has fallen in recent years, external hard drives have become popular as a means of storing files that will not fit on a computer's internal hard disc, or backing up important files. A typical external hard drive holds several hundred gigabytes of storage, and connects to the computer through the USB (universal serial bus) port.

Many users have a dedicated external hard drive that they use to store media such as pictures, music or films.

Disk access times

Programs and data are held on disks in areas called blocks, formed by the tracks and sectors and established when the disk is formatted. For a drive to read data from a disk, the read/write head must move in or out to align with the correct track (this is called the seek time). Then it must wait until the correct sector approaches the head. The total time it takes to collect the data is called the disk access time. For a hard drive the access time is around 15 milliseconds ($15/1000$ second), for floppy disks and CD-ROMs the disk access time is longer.

HINT

Note the spelling of disk/discs. Floppy and hard disks are spelt with a 'k' and compact disc with a 'c'.

Compact discs

Computer compact discs (CDs) hold up to 700 MB of data in the form of text, sound, still pictures and video clips. The data is stored as minute indentations on the surface of the disc and is read by a laser light. CDs are available in three forms:

- **CD-ROMs** – The letters ROM in the name mean read only memory. In other words, you can only read from the disc, not write or store data onto it. Software purchased on CD comes on this type of disc. The CD-ROM cannot be used for back-up as the user cannot write to the disc.

- **CD-R** – These CDs are initially blank but, using a special read/write CD drive unit, the user can store programs and data onto the disc. These discs can only be written to once.

- **CD-RW** – These are similar to the 'R' type above but the user can read, write and delete files from the disc many times, just like a hard disk.

Both CD-ROMs and CD-Rs can be referred to as WORM (**w**rite **o**nce **r**ead **m**any times) devices.

DVDs

DVD drives are now replacing CD drives in computers. DVDs have huge memory capacities, up to 17 GB. This is the equivalent capacity of 26 CDs. This capacity enables the discs to carry full-length films with subtitles and alternative soundtracks.

Drives that can write to DVD-R discs are available, although they are not as common as CD-writable drives.

DVD films

Watching a film on DVD format has advantages over VHS videotape. The digital images and soundtracks produced from the DVD are of a higher quality and the user can move to any part of the film immediately. Also the high-quality digital images do not deteriorate with constant use as they do with magnetic VHS tapes.

USB memory sticks

A USB memory stick, or 'flash drive', is a portable device that can hold large amounts of data (often between 256 MB and 4 GB). Data can be transferred to and read from them easily, and they can be carried in a pocket with no need for a protective case. However, files stored on them should be backed up elsewhere, as with any form of data storage.

Magnetic tape

Magnetic tape can also be used for permanent storage. Data is saved along the tape in blocks, separated by 'interblock gaps'. Just like the tape in a tape recorder, the data is written to or read from the tape as it passes the magnetic heads. As magnetic tape is relatively cheap, tapes are often used to take a copy of hard disks for back-up (security) reasons. One popular magnetic tape unit, of similar size to a computer hard disk unit, is called a tape streamer. These units use

tape cassettes that can store very large quantities of data, typically 400 GB. The cassettes can then be kept in a safe place away from the computer.

One disadvantage of tape storage is that you cannot go directly to an item of data on the tape as you can with a disk. It is necessary to start at the beginning of the tape and search for the data as the tape goes past the heads – this is called serial access.

Processor

The processor or central processing unit (CPU) is central to the operation of a computer. It is a very complex chip and works so hard that it needs heat sinks and fans to take away the heat it generates.

The speed at which the CPU works is determined by the computer's internal clock which generates digital pulses. Several instructions can be dealt with at once, each one moving onto the next step at each pulse of the clock. For example, at every pulse, one piece of data might be read, another might be processed, and a third might be stored into memory.

The clock speed is measured in cycles per second or Hertz. If you see a computer advertised with a '3GHz processor', this means that the clock is generating 3 000 000 000 pulses every second – so the processor is handling a lot of instructions.

Processor chip

Structure of a computer

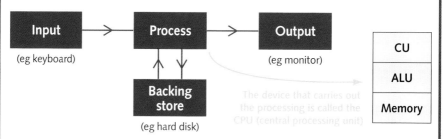

The basic operation of a computer is represented in the diagram above. Data flows from the input devices into the processor. The processor contains an arithmetic unit where number data can be added, subtracted, multiplied and divided. Instructions passed to the processor determine whether data is stored and/or passed to the output devices.

The central processing unit is made up of three parts:

- **Control unit (CU)** – The control unit manages the program instructions and opens and closes electronic gates around the computer to direct the flow of data.
- **Arithmetic and logic unit (ALU)** – This unit is where all the calculations and decisions take place.
- **Memory** – The processor contains a small amount of memory for holding data that is on its way into, or out of, the ALU. Data that is not required immediately for processing is passed out of the CPU to the RAM memory or backing store (hard disk).

Bits

Computers are constructed of electronic circuits. Through these circuits there can be two states – electricity can be flowing or not flowing. When a pulse of electricity is present we call this a '1' and the absence of electricity is a '0'. The transistors on the silicon chips can store a 'bit' (**b**inary dig**it**) which is either the 0 or the 1.

Bytes

A byte is the unit for memory in the computer. It is made up of eight bits. In other words, a byte can store eight 0s or 1s. Each character from the keyboard is given a code consisting of eight bits. These codes are the same internationally and are called the ASCII code

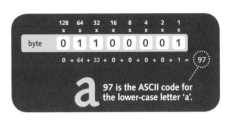

(American Standard Code for Information Interchange) ③⓪▶. The code for the letter 'a' is 97 or 01100001. Each character is held in one byte of memory. One byte is a very small amount of storage and it is more usual to refer to kilobytes (KB), megabytes (MB), gigabytes (GB) and terabytes (TB):

- 1 kilobyte = 1024 bytes (2^{10})
- 1 megabyte = 1024 kilobytes = 1 048 576 bytes (2^{20})
  - approximately 1 million bytes
- 1 gigabyte = 1024 megabytes = 1 073 741 824 bytes (2^{30})
  - approximately 1 thousand million bytes
- 1 terabyte = 1024 gigabytes = 1 099 511 627 776 bytes (2^{40})
  - approximately 1 million million bytes.

All computers have memory to store instructions and data. There are two main types of memory, random access memory (RAM) and read only memory (ROM).

RAM

The typical amount of RAM in a microcomputer might be 1 or 2 gigabytes. When the computer is switched off, this memory is empty. As the computer starts, operating instructions, computer programs and data are moved into the memory as required.

The diagram illustrates a memory map for the RAM showing how it is used to store data and programs. RAM is referred to as **volatile memory** because the content of the memory 'evaporates' when the power is switched off.

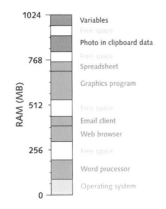

ROM

ROM is memory stored in a chip, which is not lost when the power is turned off. The ROM memory is quite small but it contains the essential instructions to enable the computer to check the hardware and operate the hard disk so that the operating system stored there can be loaded. ROM is **non-volatile memory**.

Types of computer

- Hardware is the name given to the physical parts (plastic, metal, etc) of the computer.
- Computers can be categorised into different groups depending on their size, performance and cost.
- The most powerful computers are supercomputers. These cost millions of pounds and are used for science, engineering and mathematical applications.
- Embedded computers are installed inside machines or devices.
- The basic operation of a computer is illustrated on the right:

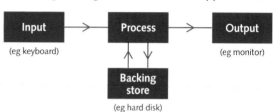

Input devices

Input devices are peripheral devices that accept data and transfer it in a digital form to the processor:

- **Keyboards** – QWERTY (standard and ergonomic), braille and concept.
- **Mouse** for controlling the screen pointer.
- **Trackerball** for controlling the screen pointer.
- **Joystick** used with computer games.
- **Graphics tablet** for art work and CAD (computer aided design).
- **Touch pad** used with notebook computers.
- **Scanner** for scanning documents and pictures.
- **Optical mark reader** (OMR) used with attendance registers, lottery forms and multiple-choice exam papers.
- **Optical character recognition** (OCR) used to read text, turnaround documents ③② and postcodes.
- **Touch screen** used with information systems in libraries, museums, etc.
- **Bar code reader** used in supermarkets, on library books, etc.
- **Light pen** for art and design work.
- **Digital camera** including Web cams, for taking digital pictures.
- **Video capture** used to take digital moving pictures.
- **Magnetic ink character recognition** (MICR) used on bank cheques.
- **Magnetic stripe** used on plastic cards.
- **Smart card** or ICC (integrated chip card) used on bank, mobile phone and satellite cards.
- **Microphone** for speech and voice input.
- **Musical instrument digital interface** (MIDI) used for creating and editing music.
- **Control** – Switches, thermistors, light-dependent resistors – sensors for data logging and control.

Output devices

Output devices are used to display or transfer data from the computer:

- **Monitors** – Traditional CRT, TFT (laptop screens and flat panel monitors), LCD (calculators) and digital projectors.
- **Printers** – Laser, ink-jet and dot-matrix – for black and colour printing.
- **Plotters** for CAD and engineers' applications.
- **Speakers** for sound and voice output.
- **Control** – Switches, actuators, LEDs – for computerised control of machines.

Process

- Data is processed in the computer by the CPU (central processing unit).
- Examples of CPUs include the Intel Core 2 Duo or the AMD Athlon chip.
- The CPU carries out software instructions, performs arithmetic operations on the data and passes data to and from the memory.

Memory

- RAM (random access memory) is formed from one or more chips inside the computer. (Typical 1 or 2 GB in a microcomputer.)
- ROM (read only memory) is a chip inside the computer that stores program instructions, normally to start (boot) the computer.
- Volatile memory means it will lose its contents when the power is switched off – RAM is volatile memory.

1 byte (8 bits)	Hold one character
1 KB	1024 bytes
1 MB	1024 KB (1 048 576 bytes)
1 GB	1024 MB (1 073 741 824 bytes)
1 TB	1024 GB (1 099 511 627 776 bytes)

Back-up storage

- Back-up storage – devices for storing data (permanent, non-volatile storage):
  - **Hard disk**
  - **CD** (compact disc)
  - **DVD**
  - **USB memory stick**
  - **Magnetic tape**
- Writable devices are available to record data to CD and DVD discs.
- ROM memory, CD-ROMs and DVD-ROMs are WORM data storage devices (WORM – write once read many times).
- The table shows the capacity and speed of back-up storage:

Device	Capacity	Data access speed*
Hard disk	120–1024 GB	Very fast
CD-ROM	700 MB	Fast
DVD-ROM	17 GB	Fast
Magnetic tape	400 GB	Very slow
USB memory stick	256 MB–4 GB	Very fast

* Includes finding (seek time) and transferring the data

A database is a collection of related data items, which are structured and linked so that the data can be accessed in a number of ways.

A database program is designed to hold information. Often, the amount of information stored is very large and it would take a long time to search through if it were written on paper. Holding the information in a database enables us to search very quickly and to sort the information easily. The required data can then be printed out as a **report**.

Two popular database programs produced by Microsoft® are:

- **Microsoft® Works** – A simple database which only uses one file or table of data. This is called a **flat file** database.
- **Microsoft® Access** – This is a more complex **relational** database that can have many tables of data with links between the tables.

Simple, flat file database

A flat file database contains one file or table of data. In the illustration below the **file** contains 100 records although only the details of the first record can be seen. Each **record**, one per student, contains seven **fields**.

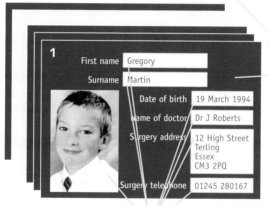

A file (table) containing 100 student records

A record – one per student

First name	Gregory
Surname	Martin
Date of birth	19 March 1994
Name of doctor	Dr J Roberts
Surgery address	12 High Street Terling Essex CM3 2PQ
Surgery telephone	01245 280167

Seven **fields** in the record

Duplicate data

In the database file above, the information about the doctor is not specific to one student – several students may have the same doctor. This means that the doctor information will be duplicated (repeated) through the records. There are disadvantages to having duplicate data:

- It takes a long time to enter the data.
- It takes up more memory storage in the computer.

If the data needs to be changed (edited), for example, an address change, this has to be carried out for every record.

Relational database

A relational database can have more than one file or table of data. In the example shown below, the same student record is displayed but the data comes from two tables. The two tables are linked through the 'Doctor code' field, as this field is in both tables. Using two tables in a relational database removes the duplication of data in the database. The details for Dr J Roberts are held just once as a record in the 'Doctor' table. If another student also has this doctor then the doctor code (ROJ1) is inserted in the student record.

Student table

Number	First name	Surname	Picture	Date of birth	Doctor code
1	Gregory	Martin	bitmap	19 March 1994	ROJ1
2	..				
100					

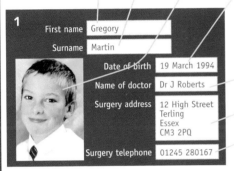

1

First name	Gregory
Surname	Martin
Date of birth	19 March 1994
Name of doctor	Dr J Roberts
Surgery address	12 High Street Terling Essex CM3 2PQ
Surgery telephone	01245 280167

Doctor table

Doctor code	Name	Address	Telephone
PHA1	...		
ROJ1	Dr J Roberts	12 High Street, Terling, Essex CM3 2PQ	01245 280167
STH1	...		

Structuring data

Structuring the data in a database enables the program to search, sort, display and print the data easily. With the data now contained in specific fields, if we wished to search for a student with a particular birth date we would start a search of the 'Date of birth' field in each record throughout the database. Structuring the data also enables us to see if a field is empty and whether or not important information is missing.

The way the database displays the information in fields makes it easier to read and easier to see if any of the important data is missing. The example illustrates this.

Student record:

Amy was born in the first week of April 1994. Her doctor, John, has his surgery in Newport Road, York and the surgery number is 351187.

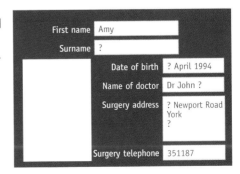

First name	Amy
Surname	?
Date of birth	? April 1994
Name of doctor	Dr John ?
Surgery address	? Newport Road York ?
Surgery telephone	351187

When designing a database it is important to select the required fields carefully. Consider the information that will be needed when the data has been entered. For example, in a database of cars you could not search for a particular colour unless a colour field had been included. Start by making a table on paper of the fields needed in your database. Divide this into columns and include the **type** of database field needed.

Boat sales example

In the example below, a database for 'Boats sales' has been designed using a variety of different field types. All the important fields have been included to enable us to sort and search the database to produce a price list or find groups or even a very specific type of boat.

Producing a table

The table lists the fields in this example database. An additional column is often included for validation checks. Validation checks are covered in 33▶.

When text fields are used, select the maximum size of the field necessary to hold the data. The different field types are described in the following illustrations.

Field name	Data type	Size	Description
Boat code	Auto number		Unique boat code number
Type	Text	2	Classification (SA = sail, MO = motor, MS = motor sailer, DI = dinghy)
Make	Text	30	Make and model
Picture	OLE object		Photograph of the boat
Description	Memo		Summary description
Construction	Text	5	Material used for boat hull (Wood, GRP, Steel, Ferro)
Length (m)	Number		Overall length (metres)
Year built	Number		Year the boat was made
Price	Currency		Price
Telephone	Text	15	Seller's telephone number
Date advertised	Date/Time		Date the boat was first advertised for sale
Under offer	Yes/No		Whether an offer has been made

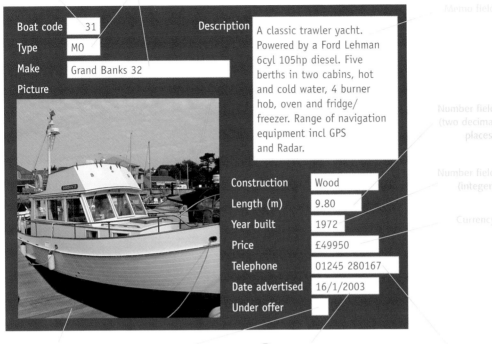

Within the form:

Boat code	31
Type	MO
Make	Grand Banks 32
Picture	
Description	A classic trawler yacht. Powered by a Ford Lehman 6cyl 105hp diesel. Five berths in two cabins, hot and cold water, 4 burner hob, oven and fridge/ freezer. Range of navigation equipment incl GPS and Radar.
Construction	Wood
Length (m)	9.80
Year built	1972
Price	£49950
Telephone	01245 280167
Date advertised	16/1/2003
Under offer	

Key fields

The key field is the one used to identify each record and is often used when searching and sorting the records. The key field contains an unique entry that no other record uses in that field.

Coding information

It is often useful to code information in database fields (31)». Advantages of this include:

- data is easier and quicker to enter
- less typing is required
- you are less likely to make spelling mistakes
- it uses less computer memory.

In the example boat database above, the types of boat have been coded as follows:

- Sail = SA
- Motor sailer = MS
- Motor = MO
- Dinghy = DI

Once a database has been designed and the data entered into the fields and records, you can search, sort and print the data.

Searching

Being able to retrieve information quickly from a database is very important. Searches are done by choosing a field and searching for a match through all the records in the database. The steps are as follows:

1 Choose the 'query' or 'find' option.

2 Specify which field in the record you wish to search.

3 Decide the condition statement (see below).

Conditions

Words	Symbols
'is equal to'	=
'is greater than'	>
'is less than'	<
'is not equal to'	< >
'is less than or equal to'	< =
'is greater than or equal to'	> =

4 Enter the value to be searched for.

5 If another condition needs to be applied to the search, go back to step 2; otherwise, start the search.

Examples

In the boat sales database shown in the previous section we could search for:

Find the boats for sale between £15 000 and £20 000

Search condition:
[Price] > 15000 AND [Price] < 20000

Results

Boat code	Make	Price
3	Gaff Cutter 35	£17 500.00
11	Hunter Horizon 26	£15 450.00
19	Westerly Griffon	£19 950.00

How many boats are made of steel?

Search condition: [Construction] = 'Steel'

Results

Boat code	Make	Construction
12	Kempala Dutch Steel	Steel

List the sailing or motor boats built after 1990 that are less than £10 000

Search condition:
([Type] = 'SA' OR [Type] = 'MO') AND [Year built] > 1990 AND [Price] < 10000

Results

Boat code	Make	Type	Year built	Price
15	Tamerisk 19	SA	1997	£7885.00

The words AND, OR and NOT used between different search statements are called **Boolean operators**. The following illustration shows how these operators work.

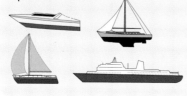

Sail AND Blue =

Sail OR Blue =

NOT Sail =

Sorting

Being able to sort the data is an important function of a database package. The steps involved in sorting data are listed below:

1. Select the first field you wish to use to sort by.

2. Decide whether the list should be in ascending (ie 'A' at the top and 'Z' at the bottom) or descending order.

3. If you wish to sort by more fields, repeat steps 1 and 2.

4. Activate the sort.

Boat code	Make	Length
5	Aqua Bell	10.00
4	Atlantic Clipper 36	11.00
15	Tamerisk 19	5.80
19	Westerly Griffon	10.70

The top and bottom of the boat list sorted by 'Make', top (ascending order), and 'Length', bottom (descending order)

Boat code	Make	Length
24	Lochin 333	19.10
29	Hartley 39	11.90
15	Tamerisk 19	5.80
16	Enterprise	3.60

Database reports

Database reports can display the data on the screen or send it to the printer. Data can be printed in columns and number fields can be totalled at the bottom of each page and at the end of the report. When designing a report, the user has a choice of which fields to display – not all the fields in the database need to be shown in the report.

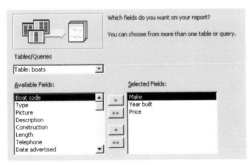

Boats

Price	Make	Year built
£199 995	Broom Ocean 38	1999
£110 000	Lochin 333	1996
£65 000	Bermudan Ketch	1965
£49 950	Grand Banks 32	1972
£49 950	Channel Islands 32	1980
£39 500	Nauticat 33	1973
£38 500	Cornish Crabber 24	1994
£34 000	Osprey	2000
£33 000	Aqua Bell	1984
£32 500	Hartley 39	1979
£32 000	Kempala Dutch Steel	1987
£30 000	Fisher 30	1973
£28 000	Fisher 25	1980
£27 500	Dolphin 31	1979

Macros

Some databases, along with other packages, have a facility to store a sequence of keystrokes and instructions. These commands are stored as a **macro**. When the instructions need to be 'replayed', the macro holding the instructions is run. Macros can reduce the time taken for repetitive tasks or make complex instructions simple to perform. For example, in a database, instructions could be stored that would search for certain records, sort them into order and print out the results. The macro containing these instructions could then be activated when the user clicks on a screen button with the mouse.

A word processor can be used to write letters, reports, essays, projects – in fact, any form of written work. When text is entered at the keyboard, the characters and words are displayed on the screen and held in the computer's memory. This work can be saved to disk and printed.

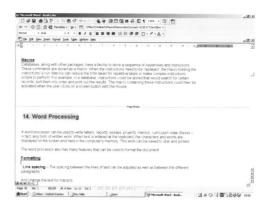

The advantage of using a word processor is that the text can be changed (edited) onscreen and reprinted if mistakes have been made. The word processor also has many features that can be used to format the document.

Formatting

When you format a document, you choose the way it looks. Characters can be **bold**, *italic*, <u>underlined</u> or CAPITAL letters. You can alter the spacing between letters and lines and you can set out writing in columns or tables.

Headers – Text placed here will automatically be printed at the top of each page, eg a chapter heading.

Margins – The area around the outside of the page which is not printed on. The size of each margin, top, bottom, left and right may be adjusted in the 'page setup'.

Bold – Making titles, subtitles, words or phrases bold will make them stand out.

Line spacing – The spacing between the lines of text can be adjusted as well as between the different paragraphs.

Bullets – Use to highlight a series of statements or a list in the document. The bullet itself can consist of any symbol but the most common is the filled circle.

Columns – Text can be placed in columns like those of a newspaper.

Fruit R' You

New twist in straight banana saga

Leeches love lychees!

Tangerine dream?

5

Footers – Text placed here will be printed at the bottom of each page, eg the page number which the word processor automatically increments through the document.

Fonts

Font is the name we give to styles of print. There are many different fonts available. You can put fonts into two groups: **serif** and **sans serif** (without serif) fonts. Serifs are the cross-strokes that cap the lines that make up a character. Serifs help the eye flow along the line as the words are read and these fonts are often used in newspapers and magazines.

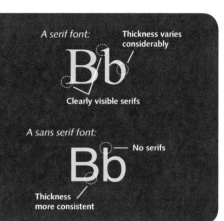

A serif font:

Thickness varies considerably

Clearly visible serifs

A sans serif font:

No serifs

Thickness more consistent

Justification

There are four ways in which text can lie in a column and you can alter all or part of the document to any one of the four. For justification, where the text is lined up to both the left- and right-hand edges, the program checks, line by line, the length of the text. If it is less than the line length, it stretches the text by spreading the letters and words, or by inserting additional spaces.

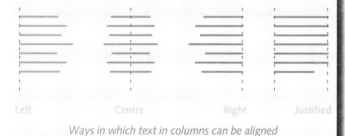

Left   Centre   Right   Justified

Ways in which text in columns can be aligned

Tabs

Tabs are often used for setting out tables or columns. Tab positions can be set across the page. When the tab key on the keyboard is pressed, the cursor (flashing bar) will jump to the next tab position across the page. The four most common types of tab markers are shown below.

Right	Centre	Left	Decimal
⬇	↓	↲	↓°
Apples	Apples	Apples	0.12
Pears	Pears	Pears	254.12
Oranges	Oranges	Oranges	1.0
Grapes	Grapes	Grapes	24.123

Orientation

Paper can be printed in two orientations, known as **portrait** and **landscape**. Portrait form, with the longer sides vertical, is the default (usual) setting. Landscape form prints with the longer sides horizontal. Landscape orientation can be useful when designing a booklet where the page will be folded, or for wide tables, illustrations and columns. The dimensions for A4 paper are: portrait 29.7 cm high by 21 cm wide; landscape 21 cm high by 29.7 cm wide.

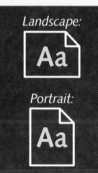

Landscape:

Aa

Portrait:

Aa

Style sheets

A style sheet holds information about the parts of a document: the body of the text, chapter titles, headings and subheadings, footers and headers, etc. Each style sheet might contain information on the font to be used, the size, alignment, spacing, colour, background, border, shading, etc. Once style sheets have been set up for a document, they are very easy to apply: highlight the particular text, eg a heading, then select the heading style from the menu list.

Heading 1	14 pt
Heading 2	12 pt
Heading 3	10 pt
• List Bullet	10 pt
Normal	10 pt

Advantages

+ It is quick to apply a range of formatting to the highlighted text.
+ With long documents, it makes it easy to be consistent, ie all the titles, subtitles, etc have the same style throughout the document.
+ Marking text with the heading style allows the word processor to create a 'contents' page automatically.
+ It makes it very easy to change formats throughout the document.

Mailmerge

Mailmerges are often used to produce personalised letters quickly. To carry out a mailmerge, you need to write a letter which contains fields that link with data from a separate source. This could be a table in a word processor, cells from a spreadsheet or, most commonly, records in a database. When the mailmerge is started, the data replaces the fields in the standard letter. A letter is produced for every database record or row of a table.

Standard letter

Data source

Department: < DEPT >

Dear < NAME >

DEPT	NAME
Maths	Mrs Crouch
History	Ms Bones
ICT	Mr Williams

Department: Maths

Department: History

Department: ICT

Dear Mr Williams

Merged letters

Personalised with names and departments

An advantage of using a word processor is that the text can be changed (edited) onscreen and reprinted if mistakes have been made.

Spell-check

The spell-checker is a useful facility for many people! It makes use of an extensive dictionary held on the disk. Each word in your document can be compared with words in the dictionary and you can change or ignore words selected by the spell-checker.

The spell-checker can suggest alternatives based on words with similar spellings or that sound similar when spoken.

Specialist dictionaries can be used for technical terms in specialist subjects like medicine. Users can also create a 'custom dictionary' to hold words they use that are not in the main dictionary. These words might include real names, address names and postcodes.

Cut and paste

Words, sentences and paragraphs can be moved around a document by using the clipboard. The section to be moved is highlighted and 'cut'. The cursor is positioned in the new location and the text returned from the clipboard using the 'paste' function.

Grammar check

The grammar check looks at the way each sentence in the document is written and compares it with a set of rules for grammar and style of writing. 'Standard' writing averages 17 words per sentence and 147 syllables per 100 words.

Modern word processors can check the spelling and grammar as the words are entered, indicating grammar errors with a green wiggly line and spelling mistakes with a red wiggly line.

This be a terribul sentence.

Thesaurus

The thesaurus is very useful when you cannot think of the right word. Select a word or phrase and the thesaurus will display a range of words with the same or similar meanings.

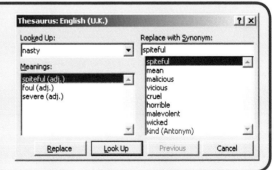

A desktop publishing (DTP) program allows you to look at the page of the document as a whole and design the layout by marking areas for text and graphics. Text can be typed directly into the DTP package or it can be imported from a word processing package. The text can be arranged in columns with large titles or headlines heading the columns. Images can be imported from graphics packages, scanned, digitised or taken from clip art libraries on disk or CD-ROM.

All these features can be put together to produce newspapers, newsletters, pages for books, posters, brochures, leaflets, prospectuses, etc.

Although modern word processors have many of the features of desktop publishing programs, they are not as fast and it is more difficult to do complex layouts on them.

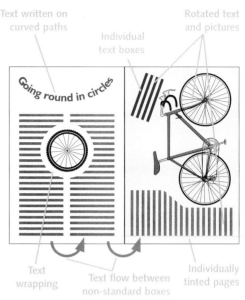

Some common features of DTP applications

Text wrapping

Often, as part of the design of a page, a graphic is placed into an area of text. You can now control the way the text and graphics interact together. The illustration below shows some of the options available. The way in which text flows around a graphic is called **text wrap**.

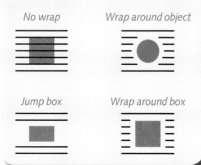

Layering

When pictures are positioned over text or text is placed over pictures in a document, this is called **layering**. In order to create the effect required, you may need to select the objects in turn and move them up or down in the 'pile'. Commands are available to 'Send to back', 'Send backward', 'Bring to front' or 'Bring forward'. You can also make the text background transparent so that the picture or image can be seen behind the text.

Graphics

Documents often require graphics, such as pictures and images, to illustrate the text. These can be imported from:

- clip art libraries
- drawing and painting packages
- scanners and digital cameras.

Once the image is displayed onscreen, you can manipulate it by resizing, rotating, shearing, cropping, etc. A full range of these manipulation techniques are illustrated below.

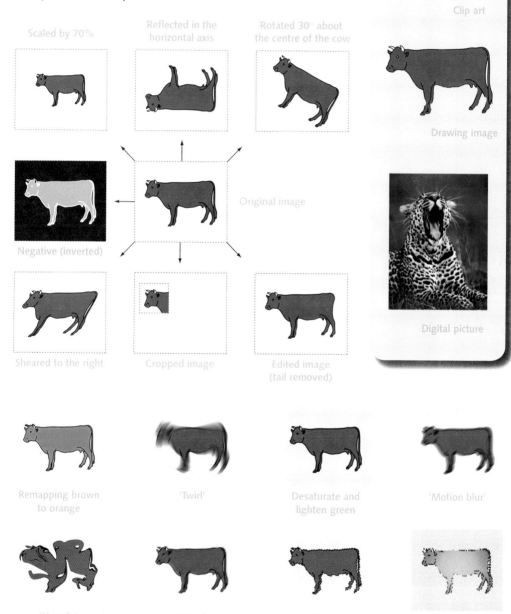

Clip art

Scaled by 70%

Reflected in the horizontal axis

Rotated 30° about the centre of the cow

Drawing image

Negative (inverted)

Original image

Digital picture

Sheared to the right

Cropped image

Edited image (tail removed)

Remapping brown to orange

'Twirl'

Desaturate and lighten green

'Motion blur'

'Liquefy'

'Pastel'

'Ripple'

'Stained glass'

There are lots of different and important uses for graphics on the computer. Drawing and painting packages are used by illustrators to create images, and games programmers use graphics to produce fast and exciting animations. Many special effects seen on television are generated through computer graphics, and computer aided design (CAD) is vital for many businesses.

Painting programs

Painting programs such as Microsoft® Paint and Adobe® Photoshop are very popular. They are called **raster** graphics packages because the image is held as a bitmap. The picture is made up of tiny picture elements called pixels (5). When you zoom into a bitmap image, the edges are often jagged and it is not always easy to rescale the picture. Bitmap images take up a lot of computer memory, as even the blank parts of the picture are stored.

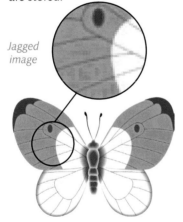

Jagged image

Drawing programs

Drawing/illustration programs, like Adobe® Illustrator, use **vector** graphics. This means that the shapes that are drawn are stored in memory as a series of instructions. This makes them easy to rescale and they take up less memory than bitmap files.

Sharp image

A mouse or a graphics tablet with a stylus can be used to create freehand drawings on the computer. Packages provide the user with a variety of brush shapes and sizes and spray tools. Colours can be selected from a palette and shapes can be flood filled. All, or part, of a selected drawing can be moved or copied and manipulated on the screen by reflection, rotation, shearing, scaling and cropping (16).

Clip art

Programs, like the Microsoft® Office collection, come with their own library of professionally-prepared graphics which can be used in documents and publications. You can also buy CDs containing clip art.

Computer aided design (CAD)

CAD packages are used by designers, engineers and scientists to design many things including buildings, cars, chemical plants, circuit boards, computers and machinery. CAD software is often complex and requires powerful computers to run it.

Computer aided design packages have many special features. These include:

- displaying a three-dimensional, 'solid' version of an object
- displaying a rotating object from different angles
- 'suggesting' suitable materials for constructing an object to provide the strength and flexibility required
- calculating the stresses and strains in a structure and warning the designer of weaknesses
- simulating and testing a design, for example, testing the operation of an electronic circuit board with inputs and outputs.

Using CAD software enables drawings to be done more quickly. Changes can

be made without having to start the whole drawing again and parts of drawings that are needed more than once can be copied. Many companies have large libraries of drawings held on disk which can be retrieved and modified very rapidly. Fine detail can be achieved by zooming in on the drawing, and the tedious task of shading can be done automatically.

Using a computer network, a number of designers can work on the same project at the same time and employees throughout the company, from the board room to the shop floor, can access drawings via their workstations to assist them with their work and decision-making.

Computer aided manufacture (CAM)

Computer aided manufacture is a process of aiding production in manufacturing companies by using computers to operate machines. Some machines shape materials; four common processes are lathing, milling, drilling and pressing. Other machines transport the goods between one process and the next, and computer-controlled robot arms may be involved in spraying paint or welding joints.

CAD/CAM

The most effective method of production is to design products using a computer aided design package and then pass

instructions directly from this package to the machines which are manufacturing the product. Data from the design software is translated into instructions for guiding the lathes, milling and drilling machines and presses. This whole process is fully automated. The introduction of these systems into the manufacturing industry has:

- resulted in faster manufacture as machine settings are made directly from the design plans
- reduced the demand for machine operators
- created a demand for skilled computer operators.

A presentation package allows you to prepare and give presentations using a computer. The information being presented is made into a set of **slides**. Each slide can contain text, clip art, graphics, video, sound and/or animation. Microsoft® PowerPoint, which is part of the Microsoft® Office suite of programs, is a popular presentation software package.

Presentation packages are used for many different purposes:

- A saleswoman might use the program to demonstrate a new product.
- A teacher might use it to give a lesson or lecture.
- A student might use the software to prepare a talk for a school assembly.

In business

Presentations are quite common in the business world. These might be to customers, clients or others in the company. Presentation packages can assist the user by offering complete sets of slides for different types of presentation. The user only has to edit the detail on each slide for their own product or company. Common uses for presentations include:

- business plans
- company meetings
- marketing meetings
- organisational structures
- sales presentations
- technical product presentations.

Animation

Animation helps to give presentations more impact. In Microsoft® PowerPoint, the change from one slide to the next can be animated in over 40 different ways. For example, the new slide can appear by moving across the old slide from the side or bottom. This can be accompanied by selected sounds. You can make text and graphics appear separately through animation: words and pictures can 'drive' in or 'fly' onto the slide; individual letters can be projected onto the slide as if by a laser beam, or appear as if they were printed by a typewriter.

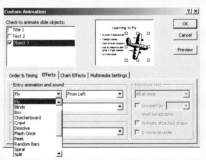

There are many different animations to use

Preparing a presentation

Before starting work on the computer, it is a good idea to draft your ideas for each slide on paper. When this has been done, you can choose the best layout and design for each slide from a selection offered in the program. You then need to add text, graphics, sound and animation to complete the presentation.

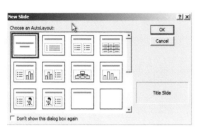

1 Choose a suitable layout for your slide.

2 Type in the title and text.

3 Select a picture from your clip art library, or scan one in.

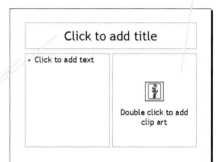

If the audience needs more detail, this can be added as notes and printed out, with a copy of the slide, for them to take away afterwards.

4 The finished slide.

Giving a presentation

When you use a program like Microsoft® PowerPoint to make a presentation, use the key points displayed on each slide and talk to the audience giving them more detail. Project your voice to the back of the audience; be enthusiastic, relaxed and confident. Try to smile and make eye contact and speak clearly, using pauses to emphasise points.

Creating Web pages

When you visit a site on the Internet, the Web pages you see are created using HTML (HyperText Markup Language). This is not a programming language but a set of codes that enable you to format the page and link to other pages and sites.

HTML commands are called tags and are enclosed by < and >. These tags are often paired, one to start a command and one to finish it. An example of HTML tags is shown on the right.

Pages written in HTML code can be read by Web browsers. One of the most common browsers is Microsoft® Internet Explorer, which comes with the Microsoft® Windows operating system. Another popular browser is Mozilla Firefox. HTML files are stored as long unbroken strings of ASCII ⑨▸ characters that can be transmitted easily across the Web. These files have extensions to their file names of .htm or .html.

To start an HTML document, insert a title called "GCSE Information Technology" and write some information, the code would be:

<html>	Tells the browser that this is an HTML document
<head>	The 'head' of an HTML document can contain extra information about the document, including its title
<title>	Tells the browser the title of the Web page
GCSE Information Technology	
</title>	The forward slash / closes the tag command
</head>	Closes the 'head' tag
<body>	The 'body' of an HTML document will contain the main text
This is where the information should go.	
</body>	Closes the 'body' tag
</html>	Closes the 'html' tag and therefore comes at the end of the document

HTML tags

Many different tags are available to format a page. Tags can alter the size of text, produce horizontal lines across the page and make text **bold**, *italic* and <u>underlined</u>. Tags can add colour, insert images, tables, lists, bullet points, indents and can alter borders and fonts. Special tags, called anchor tags <A>, use hypertext reference commands and create links to other pages or sites. This is illustrated below.

<A HREF = "http://www.example.sch.uk/home.html"> Go to home page </A>

This anchor tag and hypertext reference example will take the user to the home page.

Other tags allow users of the Web page to make choices by selecting menu choices, radio buttons and ticking check boxes. Users can also type in text boxes.

Inserting images

Images can make a Web page more interesting but they can also slow down the speed a page takes to appear on the screen. Image files are created in different formats and two popular ones used with Web page design are GIFs and JPEGs:

- GIFs (graphics interchange format) are good for non-photographic images. They are limited to 256 colours.

- JPEGs (joint photographic experts group) are good for photographs. This type of image can lose some detail although it is hard to spot. JPEG images can have 16.7 million colours.

Web site design

There are two parts to designing a Web site. The first is to design the structure of the whole site, how many pages will be used and how they link together. The second part of the design process is to create the Web page in an interesting and informative way.

Linking pages

Start by deciding what pages are necessary in your Web site. Sketch the layout of the pages on paper and complete the links between the pages (known as hyperlinks).The illustration below shows the page links for a local club site on the Internet.

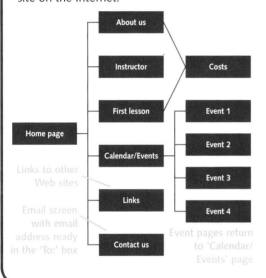

Page design

When your Web pages are uploaded to the Internet, they will be in competition with millions of other sites. Your pages need to be attractive, interesting, easy to use (or navigate) and fast to load. Start by considering what the page needs to achieve and then consider the following questions:

- Will this objective be easier to achieve using pictures?
- Is the page content and design suitable for your expected audience?
- Are there links to other key pages?
- Have you checked for spelling and grammar errors?
- Do the different pages have a similar layout (template) and use of colour?

When writing an article, start with the main details. This can be done by answering the questions: Who? Why? What? When? Where?

Software packages

You do not need to know HTML to create Web pages. Packages like Microsoft® FrontPage and Macromedia Dreamweaver allow users to design pages and then create links between the pages. The programs then create the HTML code automatically. These programs are called WYSIWYG (What You See Is What You Get) because they display a formatted version of the page as you edit. However, unlike a desktop publishing program, the resulting pages will not appear exactly the same in all browsers .

Advertising your Web site

Once you have uploaded your Web site to the Internet, as well as keeping it updated, you need to advertise it. Internet search engines have automated 'Web crawlers' that are always looking for new sites and will insert the key words from your site into their databases. With so many sites, this process can take a long time. Other ways of advertising include:

- Adding the Web address (URL) to your email signature so it appears on every email you send.
- Asking other people with Web sites to add a link to your site.
- Registering the site with the Internet search engines .

A spreadsheet is a computer program designed to display and process numbers. It is made up of a grid into which numbers are entered. The program contains many mathematical, statistical and financial calculations which can be applied to the numbers. Many spreadsheets can also show the numbers in the form of graphs. Microsoft® Excel, which comes as part of Microsoft® Office, is one of the most widely-used spreadsheets.

A spreadsheet is a powerful tool for experimenting with different mathematical models. For example, a salesman might decide to reduce the price of his products to sell more. A spreadsheet can be used to see how many extra sales are needed to make the same profit for different price reductions.

'What if...?'

'What if…?' is a phrase often associated with spreadsheets. If a number in one cell is changed, then the value in another cell may also change if it uses the first number in a calculation. This may change a third cell, and so on. This means that by altering the content of individual cells, you can investigate quite complex changes instantly. For example, what would be the effect on a company's profit if we reduced prices by 4%, increased sales by 5% and increased staff wages by 6%?

Spreadsheet cells

Cells in the spreadsheet may contain numbers, text (letters, words, etc), dates and formula. Each cell, or block of cells, may be formatted so that the content of the cells are displayed in different ways. When a formula is used in a cell then the result of the calculation is displayed in the cell while the original formula can be seen in the 'formula bar' above the spreadsheet when the cell is selected.

Calculations

The power of a spreadsheet comes from its ability to do calculations with numbers. The content of one cell can be calculated from other cells in the sheet. For example, suppose you want the content of cell C2 to equal A2 multiplied by B2. Instead of typing a value into C2, the formula $= A2*B2$ can be entered. If the number in A2 or B2 is changed, the new answer will automatically be calculated in cell C2.

Making a chart

Highlight the data in the spreadsheet that is required for the chart. This should include the text headings, as these will become the axis labels. Select the Chart Wizard icon 📊. Follow the four steps in the wizard.

HINT

If the data items you wish to chart are not in rows or columns next to each other, highlight one set of data, then, holding down the CTRL key (lower left of the keyboard) select the other data set. Holding down the CTRL keys stops the first set of data from losing its highlighted status.

Spreadsheets

20

Formulae and functions

Spreadsheet packages come with an extensive library of formulae and functions. The majority of spreadsheet users only use a small percentage of those available. In the library there are formulae and functions for:

- financial calculations, eg to calculate repayments on a loan
- handling dates and times, eg to work out the day of the week from the date
- mathematical and trigonometry, eg to find the cosine of an angle
- statistical work, eg to calculate the standard deviation
- logical expressions, eg to return a value if a statement is true.

This example shows two spreadsheet functions – the **SUM** function and the

	A	B	C	D	E	F	G
			Paper 1	Paper 2	Paper 3	Total	Pass/Fail
1			(30%)	(30%)	(40%)	(%)	(45%)
2							
3	Katie	NORMAN	12	14	20	46	Pass
4	Noel	LUFF	4	5	15	24	Fail
5	Caroline	KELL	1	19	27	47	Pass
6	Laura	WOOLEY	9	13	30	52	Pass
7	Matthew	JONES	13	9	17	39	Fail

IF statement. The spreadsheet shows the results of an examination. The pass mark is 45% and the formulae in the right-hand column show whether the student has passed or failed.

The cell coloured   has the formula **=SUM(C4:E4)**.
This adds the contents of cells C4 to E4, ie $4 + 5 + 15 = 24$.

The cell coloured ■ has the function **= IF(F4>45,"Pass","Fail")**.
This means 'If the content of Cell F4 is greater than 45 then display "Pass", otherwise display "Fail"'. 24 is less than 45, so the cell shows "Fail".

Columns F and G contain formulae. After the formula has been entered into one cell, it can be copied down or across the sheet to other cells. When it is copied, the references to other cells also change. For example, the formula = SUM(C4:E4), when copied down to the cell in the row below, becomes = SUM(C5:E5). This process is called **replication**.

Graphs and charts

An important feature of a spreadsheet is to plot the values in the sheet as a graph or chart. Seeing figures in graphical form often makes it easier to see trends in the values. Some of the chart types available in Microsoft® Excel are:

Column chart	How data changes over time or comparisons between different items. Can be two- or three-dimensional.
Bar chart	Horizontal bars for comparisons between different items. (Note: Bar charts in mathematics textbooks are column charts in Excel.)
Line charts (graphs)	Shows the trend in data. Data is shown at equal intervals along the horizontal axis.
Area charts	Emphasise the size of the change in data with time. The total is shown together with all the contributing parts.
Pie charts	These are circular charts with each data item forming a slice of the circle. Slices can be pulled out of the 'pie' to emphasise their importance.
XY (scatter) chart	Used for scientific and mathematical data and shows the relationships between sets of data.

Modelling

Modelling is when a computer program attempts to represent a real situation using mathematical equations. Different values can be input to the model to investigate possible outcomes. These inputs can be imaginary values or they can be real values from data collection instruments and sensors.

Weather forecasting is a good example of computer modelling. Although there is evidence that forecasting dates back 3000 years, it was not until 1922 that the first mathematical model was proposed. This model could not be used though, as the calculations were too difficult to complete by hand and the computer had not been invented!

Weather modelling

Instruments are constantly gathering weather data. These include weather stations, weather balloons, cameras on orbiting satellites, special radar stations and instruments on boats and aeroplanes. This data is input into a supercomputer that has 700 processing units, each capable of performing 600 million calculations every second. This massive operation is not done simply to inform us that it might be sunny tomorrow when we might be planning to take a day out to the seaside! Many organisations rely on accurate forecasts to plan their operations. These include airlines, shipping companies, fishermen, sailors, farmers and the environment agency who are responsible for issuing flood warnings.

Today, the weather centre in Exeter uses an NEC SX 6/8 supercomputer, one of the most powerful computers in Europe, for weather forecasting.

Computer models are used to investigate the effect of:

- flooding
- global warming
- economic growth and recession
- radiation spread from nuclear accidents or attacks.

A supercomputer

A computer spreadsheet can be used as a modelling program. Different outputs are generated by the functions and formulae in the spreadsheet when changes are made to key values. For example, when taking out a mortgage to purchase a house, the monthly repayments depend on the interest rate over the period of the loan. A spreadsheet can be used as a model to show repayments for different interest rates.

Simulation

Civil aircraft flight simulator (interior)

A simulation program is designed to predict the likely behaviour of a real-life system which is represented as a mathematical model. A flight simulator is a good example of a simulation program. These are used to train pilots and consist of full-size cockpits mounted on hydraulic legs. Computer screens are positioned in place of windows and these display lifelike images that change according to the movement of the aircraft through the controls.

Although simulators are very expensive, they are still really useful when training pilots.

Benefits include:

+ they are much less expensive to operate than an actual aeroplane
+ training is not affected by weather conditions
+ emergency situations can be simulated
+ conditions, such as night flying, can be simulated
+ take-offs and landings can be practised at airports around the world.

Even simulators sold for home use, like the Microsoft® Flight Simulator, are sophisticated programs that can assist students studying for their private pilot's licence. This program includes interactive air traffic control, flight analysis, a range of aircraft to fly and detailed scenery over towns and cities.

Civil aircraft flight simulator (exterior)

In schools, simulation software for different subject areas allows students to investigate experiments and processes. Using simulations on a computer enables students to:

• revise work done in class
• experiment safely with dangerous materials
• study in their own time and at their own pace
• extend their studies for greater understanding.

> Warning! A computer simulation is only as good as the rules the computer programmer has used to represent the real-life event. Remember, it may have limitations.

Data logging is when you capture and store data to use at a later time. Sensors are used to input the data which is then stored in memory. This data can be displayed in graphs and tables or passed to a spreadsheet program for analysis. Data logging is particularly important in scientific experiments.

LogIT Explorer in use measuring sound, light and temperature

Sensors

There are sensors to measure light, heat, sound, movement, pressure, radiation, acidity, humidity and the strains and stresses in materials. The more common sensors are:

- **Light sensors** – Eg light-dependent resistor (LDR). As the light intensity increases, the electrical resistance of the LDR decreases allowing more electricity to flow through the device.
- **Heat sensors** – Eg thermistor. As the temperature increases, the electrical resistance of the thermistor decreases allowing more electricity to flow through the device.
- **Switches** – Eg light gate switch. This switch is often used to start and stop timers. As an object passes through the light gate, the beam is broken causing the switch to activate.

Converting sensor readings for input to the computer

Most sensors, including the light and heat sensors referred to above, produce an analogue output. This means that they generate a variable signal, from low to high, like the volume control on a radio. Computers operate using digital signals. An 'analogue to digital converter' is required to convert the signal from the sensor into the digital pulses (0s and 1s) for the computer.

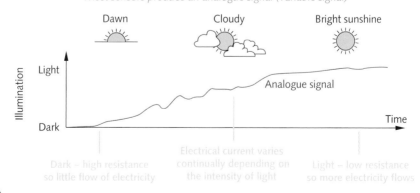

Most sensors produce an analogue signal (variable signal)

Dawn   Cloudy   Bright sunshine

Analogue signal

Illumination

Light

Dark

Time

Dark – high resistance so little flow of electricity

Electrical current varies continually depending on the intensity of light

Light – low resistance so more electricity flows

Why use data logging?

There are many advantages of using data logging equipment in experiments:

+ Data loggers can record measurements with great accuracy.

+ Taking a reading may interfere with the experiment; for example, inserting a thermometer to measure the temperature of a liquid may allow heat to escape. However, data logging sensors can be sealed inside the equipment.

Scientist with microclimate data logger from British Antarctic Survey

+ Data loggers can collect large amounts of data measurements over very short periods of time. For example, taking hundreds of measurements during a chemical reaction lasting less than a second.

+ Data loggers can collect data measurements unattended over very long periods of time. For example, equipment could be set to record the growth of a plant, taking measurements every hour for months.

+ Data loggers can operate in environments which would be hostile to people. Equipment can be designed to operate in orbiting satellites, the depths of the oceans, in deserts or the Arctic or Antarctic.

Calibrating sensors

To ensure that readings from sensors are meaningful and accurate they must be calibrated. To calibrate a heat sensor, the electrical current flowing through the device is measured at known temperatures. In the example shown, the current is 1 amp at 0°C and 3 amps at 100°C. From this the software could calculate all the points in between, for example, a current of 2 amps would be 50°C.

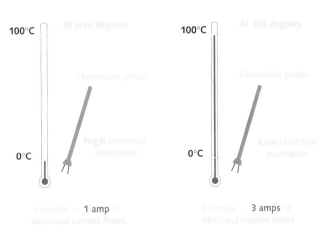

Sensor design

Sensors must be designed for the environment in which they will be used. For example, if you want a sensor to record the depth of a river, it must be waterproof! In chemical plants, the equipment might have to be resistant to acids and alkalis. Data logging equipment and any on-board computer equipment in an orbiting satellite would need to work in a vacuum, with extremes of temperature and radiation.

Computers are used to control the operation of many machines and everyday objects. The computer program's instructions send signals from the computer to devices like switches and motors which make the machine operate correctly.

Embedded computers

When a computer is used to control a machine, a computer circuit board is installed inside the machine. Input sensors and output control devices are then connected to these circuits; this is an embedded computer. The computer control program is written using a 'normal' computer and downloaded to a ROM chip (permanent memory) into the embedded computer. Embedded computers in control systems must use 'real-time' processing ⑳ in order to respond immediately to incoming data.

Input devices

Switches and sensors are used as input devices in computer control. Switches can be activated by the user, for example, when selecting the 'type of wash' on a washing machine, or by some movement during the process. The sensors used include ones to monitor temperature, light levels, pressure and sound.

Output devices

The most important output device is a **switch**. Switches can start and stop electrical devices like heaters, pumps and motors. Often the tiny output signals from the computer need to be amplified to switch these devices so special electronic components called silicon controlled rectifiers (SCRs) are used to boost the signal. A particular type of motor called a **stepper motor** ⑦ is controlled directly by signals from the computer. In order to show the user how the control program is progressing, LCDs (liquid crystal displays) and LEDs (light-emitting diodes) are used.

Washing machine

Inputs: Water flow sensors, water level sensors, temperature sensors, panel switches, door open switch, spin speed selector.

Process:
Stored programs for different wash cycles, eg woollens, cotton, etc. Each program controls the water  temperature and level, and the timing and sequence of the wash, rinse and spin cycles.

Outputs: Switches to operate water pumps and valves, water heaters, the drum motor and indicator lights.

Camera

Inputs: Light sensor, push buttons, film speed sensor, battery power and end of film sensor.

Process: Calculate light level and adjust shutter speed and aperture (size of hole allowing light in) according to film speed. Calculate focus points to produce a sharp image. Activate motor to wind film on and draw back shutter for the next picture. Activate flash if necessary.

Outputs: Shutter actuator, memory storage, lens focusing motor, LCD display, flash.

Control 'bit' patterns

The pattern of binary digits (bits) from the computer is used to control the output devices. The illustration shows how bits 2 and 3 are controlling a motor.

Eight 'control' bits

7	6	5	4	3	2	1	0
1	0	0	1	1	0	0	1

Control motor 1

Bit 2 – 1 = Forward, 0 = Reverse

Bit 3 – 1 = On, 0 = Off

Why use computer control in manufacturing?

Although the initial cost of installing computerised machines in factories is high, there are many benefits that make their use essential for companies to run their businesses competitively 48 .

Feedback

In computer control, feedback means that input signals produce output changes that are monitored again by the input sensors. There is a loop from the sensor, through the processor to the output and back to the sensor. The flow-chart shows a feedback loop. Here, a computer-controlled vehicle is moving into position to stack goods on a shelf in a warehouse. The input sensor switch is mounted at the front of the truck and the output is the forward motor.

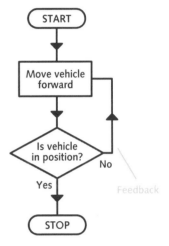

Actuators

An actuator 7 is any device which can be operated by signals from a computer to generate physical movement. These include:

- **Hydraulics** – Here the output from the computer controls the movement of hydraulic rams by pumping oil. These hydraulic rams are very powerful.
- **Pneumatics** – Pneumatics are similar to hydraulics in using rams, but the pistons are powered by air rather than oil. Pneumatics are not as powerful as hydraulic systems but the movements can be very fast.
- **Motors** – Electrical motors can be switched on or off by the computer and can drive cogs, gears, wheels and pumps to operate mechanisms. A stepper motor operates directly from the computer and turns an exact amount, for example 1.8°, for each digital pulse from the computer. This very precise movement makes stepper motors ideal for computer printers and plotters.

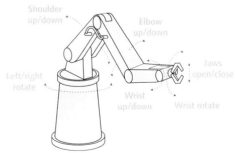

Industrial robot showing the six degrees of freedom

A computer without any programs is of little use to anyone. It is the software running on the computer that makes it useful and fun to use. All software, from desktop publishing programs to the latest games, is written using a programming language. These languages enable programmers to write the instructions, or commands, that make up a computer program.

Different languages

A variety of languages can be used to write programs, each with its own strengths. Programmers therefore choose the most appropriate language to use for the task. Common languages include:

- **BASIC** (Beginners All-purpose Symbolic Instruction Code) – Originally used to teach computer programming, now replaced by Visual Basic and VBA (Visual Basic for Applications). Used in Microsoft® Access and Excel.

- **Visual Basic** – A popular language using a Windows environment, ideal for learning computer programming but also very powerful.

- **Cobol** (Common Business Orientated Language) – Used to develop business software, it has good file handling and in-built financial routines.

- **Fortran** (Formula Translation) – Used for scientific and engineering applications; contains many built-in mathematical functions and handles numbers with great speed.

- **C++** – Popular for modern commercial software.

- **Java** – A modern language ideal for use with the Internet.

Some basic programming techniques

- **Variables, sums and counters** – A variable is a part of the memory we can give a label to, eg the letter 'A'. Variables can hold numbers or words. In the example opposite the store is holding numbers. Note that here the equals sign ' = ' has quite a different meaning to when it is used in mathematics.

A = 3	Put 3 into variable 'A'.
B = A + 4	Add 4 to the number in 'A' and place the total in variable 'B'.
A = A + 1	A counter – add 1 to contents of 'A', then place the total back into variable 'A'.

- **Loops** – It is often necessary to perform a task several times, so a loop is used. If we know how many times we need to repeat instructions, we use a 'For … Next … ' loop.

```
For A = 1 to 10
  Print A
Next A
```

A loop – 1 is placed in 'A', when the instruction 'Next A' is reached the program jumps back to the first line and 2 is placed into 'A'. This continues until 'A' = 10.

- **Decisions** – Two or more values are compared using the = (equals), > (greater than) or < (less than) operators. If the statement is true then one set of instructions are carried out, if false, a different set are performed.

If A = 1234 Then open_lock

If the number in variable 'A' is equal to 1234 then the instructions in a subprogram called 'open-lock' are activated.

Program flow charts

These are used to show the operations involved in a computer program. Different symbols are used to represent particular operations. Flow charts can be constructed before the program instructions are written to help the programmer, or they can be drawn afterwards to help document the program. Documentation is important to help other users understand how the program works so that future maintenance can take place.

Symbol	Description
Connector	Used when a flow chart continues on the next page.
Terminator	Used for 'start' and 'stop'.
Input/output	Used to show input and output of data.
Decision	Used to illustrate different paths being taken based on decisions. Decision boxes can have more than two exits.
Process	Used to represent a sequence of instructions or operations not involving a decision.
Subroutine	Used to indicate a sequence of instructions which will have its own flow chart elsewhere.

Example of a program flow chart

The flow chart illustrates graphically the sequence of control instructions required to open a security door. A numeric keypad with a pass code of '1324' unlocks the door, but if more than three wrong codes are entered, an alarm is triggered.

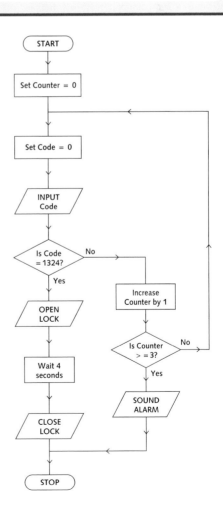

Algorithms

Computer programs are written to perform tasks on the computer. The programmer has to work out a set of software instructions to complete the task. This sequence of steps is called an algorithm. Larger software projects may contain many different algorithms.

All computers use an operating system (OS). This is a complex program, with millions of software instructions, that controls the operation of the computer.

It handles the:

- input, such as data, from the keyboard
- output to the screen
- transfer of data to and from the disk drives.

A good operating system should make the computer easy to operate and, at the same time, ensure that the powerful hardware is used fully.

The Windows 2000 operating system

Methods of operation

Operating systems are designed to cater for different needs. Modern operating systems can handle many different tasks simultaneously. These are described as follows:

- **Single program mode** – Just one program runs on the computer at a time. Some of the smaller operating systems running on hand-held devices work in this way.

- **Multi-tasking (multi-program) mode** – Two or more programs can be run at once. The operating system ensures that the resources of the computer are shared, including the processor where each program shares the processor time. Running a word processor and a spreadsheet together in Windows is an example of multi-tasking.

- **Multi-user mode** – Several users can use the same system together and the operating system gives each user a share of processor time. Two people logging onto the network at the same time is an example of multi-user operation.

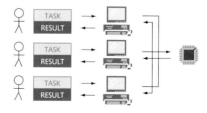

Examples of three operating systems are:

- **UNIX** – This was written in the computing language C and can handle many users (multi-user) and many tasks (multi-tasking) at the same time. UNIX was originally designed for mainframe computers.
- **Microsoft® Windows XP** – A popular operating system used on desktop computers in homes, schools and businesses.
- **Microsoft® Windows 2003 Server** – A more complex multi-tasking operating system used in network environments.
- **Microsoft® Windows Vista** – The most recent version of Windows, designed to be more secure and easier to use.

Although the illustrations below show different features of operating systems, practical systems combine these features. For example, a sophisticated OS could handle multiprocessors, users and tasks simultaneously.

- **Multi-processor mode**
  – In larger systems, the computer contains more than one processor. The operating system allows the different processors to operate together and share 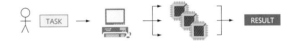 the same memory. The operating system may split a large job into parts and share them between the processors or it may allocate each processor its own complete job.

- **Batch processing mode** – It is sometimes more efficient to collect together a group of data, and then run this  through the computer in one go rather than running the program as each piece of data is entered. This is called batch processing as the data is collected as a batch. An example of batch processing is running a payroll program. The wages data (eg hours worked) is batched together before the program is run to calculate the monthly wages. During batch processing, there is no user input.

- **Real-time** – The computer reacts immediately to incoming data and responds with outputs  straightaway. These inputs might come from remote sensors, for example, an aeroplane running on automatic pilot. A change to the plane's flight caused by air currents must be corrected immediately. Another example of real-time processing is making a reservation for the cinema or for a coach trip. When reserving the seat, the computer blocks others from taking the same seats even if they enquire a second later. Computers running in real-time must be fast enough and have enough processing power to handle extreme situations.

An operating system is a complex program. Some of the tasks it needs to perform to ensure the efficient operation of the computer system include:

- allocating a slice of time with the processor for each job that needs to be processed
- ensuring that jobs with different priorities are dealt with in the correct order
- creating a balance between tasks which require a lot of processing time and tasks needing more use of peripherals, eg printers
- handling input and output (sometimes abbreviated to just i/o) and ensuring that input goes to the right program and output goes to the correct place
- maximising the use of the computer's memory by allocating different sections to the programs and data being used
- maintaining system security, for example, allowing the administrator user full control but other users only access to running the file, not changing or deleting it
- providing a friendly and easy-to-use interface for users.

Command line interface

It is possible to give the computer instructions without the aid of menus and icons. To do this you must leave the Windows environment. Instructions can then be typed directly into the computer so that they can be seen onscreen. This has the disadvantage that the user must know the commands to type in. The advantage is that quite specific and powerful instructions can be given directly.

To view a command line interface in Windows XP – click on 'Start', 'Programs', 'Accessories' and 'Command Prompt'; in Windows 98 – click on 'Start', 'Programs' and then 'MS-DOS Prompt'. To exit, type 'exit' and press the 'Enter' key.

Command to display files in a directory

Results of operation

Command to copy a file from the hard disk onto a storage device

```
C:\MYFILES>dir
 Volume in drive C has no label.
 Volume Serial Number is E81E-6E42

 Directory of C:\MYFILES

17/12/2007  11:20       <DIR>          .
17/12/2007  11:20       <DIR>          ..
17/12/2007  11:12               19,456 Homework.doc
17/12/2007  11:13               19,456 letter.doc
17/12/2007  11:14               13,824 TEAM.xls
               3 File(s)         52,736 bytes
               2 Dir(s)  75,645,198,336 bytes free

C:\MYFILES>copy letter.doc z:
        1 file(s) copied.
```

Human–computer interface

The way in which a computer user communicates with the computer is called the human–computer interface (or man–machine interface). In the early days of computing there were no keyboards and monitors. Data was input using punched cards and paper tape and the output was printed to a machine like a typewriter. A user of these systems had to be a computer expert. Modern operating systems make it easy for users of all abilities to use a computer.

A good interface between the user and the computer program should be:

- friendly – being able to use the software without needing to read the whole manual first
- attractive – uses colour well and encourages users to use the software
- effective – it does the job it is designed to do efficiently
- easy to use – menu structures are consistent across packages.

One form in common use is the **graphical user interface** or **GUI** system (pronounced 'gooey'). Small pictures or icons representing actions are displayed and can be selected with the mouse. The use of windows makes the operation of programs easier. Another term used for this form of interface is **WIMP** (windows, icons, menus and pointer).

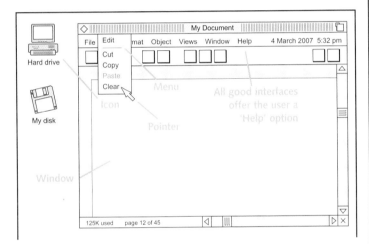

Sometimes the menu choices appear 'grey' or 'ghosted' and cannot be selected. For example, the paste command in the edit menu cannot be used until data has been passed to the clipboard using the cut or copy commands. The screen may display several windows for different applications but only the one currently in use will be active.

A great deal of time, thought and research goes into the design of the screen layout. It is important to make all the facilities of the computer available to the user but not to clutter the desktop, making it difficult to use. Both operating systems and application programs give the user the option to customise the screen to suit their preferences. Icons and folders can be added or removed and menus and tool bars can be changed to personalise the desktop.

Consistency is also important. This means for example that if the print option is in the file menu in the word processor then you would also find it in the file menu when using a spreadsheet.

Software development in business

In business, the process of introducing a new computerised system is given the name 'system life cycle'. The stages in the cycle are similar to those used in your coursework but the evaluation stage is replaced with a maintenance stage. This stage makes sure that the system continues to operate correctly in daily use and fixes any bugs that come to life after extensive use. The maintenance stage may continue for many years but

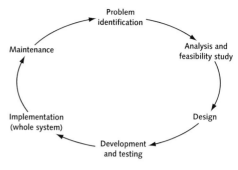

System life cycle

eventually major modifications or new systems will be required – this is the reason it is shown as a cycle. There are differences in opinion about the exact number and description of the stages in the system's life cycle.

Analysis

This stage should show that you understand the way that the task is currently done and that you have carried out a feasibility study to show that an ICT solution is the right approach. It is not possible to design software for a user unless you understand their requirements. To find this information, you could:

- interview or ask the person(s) doing the task to complete a questionnaire
- observe the way the task is currently being done and make notes
- collect and study the data, forms, screen displays, printouts currently in use.

The results should be included in your project write-up as evidence. After a detailed examination of the problem, look at whether a computerised solution is the right approach. Will it reduce paperwork, speed up the processing, give better stock control, create fewer mistakes, and provide better reports for the managers? Will these potential benefits outweigh the costs involved in introducing the new system? It should be clear that the answer to this question is 'Yes' before proceeding. Use the following checklist to help you:

- Identify a task which will make sensible use of the ICT tools. ☐
- Gather information about the task. ☐
- Define the problem. ☐
- Who are the potential users? Gather their views. Use a questionnaire or interview. ☐
- Produce a design specification to include all aspects of the task, including resources. ☐
- Show the flow of data through the system with a data flow diagram (28▶). ☐
- What are the limitations of the potential users? Would they be able to manage your proposed system? ☐
- What are the limitations imposed by the resources available? Consider equipment, software packages and peripherals. ☐
- Outline the objectives for the project. ☐
- Specify the data sources required for the task. ☐

GCSE coursework

For your GCSE coursework you are required to do projects where ICT is used to assist in a variety of tasks. For example, this might involve creating a spreadsheet or database or designing a control program. Whether a project is required in school or in business the development process follows a similar structured process. This process is illustrated below.

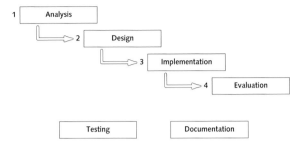

Testing and documentation must also be included, either as separate stages, or as part of the ones above.

When you write up your project you should include details for each of the stages. You should also include sketches and diagrams, tables, graphs, flow charts, printouts and photographs where appropriate to enhance your work.

Design

There are several methods of designing a solution for a chosen problem. A popular method is a 'top-down design' approach. Starting with the main task, this is broken down into sub-tasks. These sub-tasks are then divided further to show more detail. An example of a top-down approach is shown in the illustration on the right.

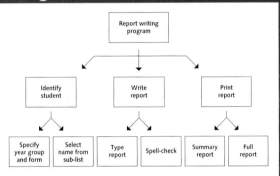

Top-down design in operation for a computer program to write reports for students

- Look at a range of different solutions using different methods and software packages. ☐
- Consider the computer versus the non-computer solution and the effect of resources on the chosen design. ☐
- Choose one solution and justify the choice. ☐
- Show with flow charts how the proposed solution will operate. ☐
- Ensure that the chosen design proposal matches the requirements of the potential users. ☐
- Describe the structure and quantity of input data required and the output from the system. ☐
- Show the design of forms, reports and queries that might be used in the system. ☐
- Explain if validation and verification of data are required/used in the solution. ☐
- Design a comprehensive test strategy for the system (28). ☐

Note: Depending on the examination board you are using, the structure may alter slightly. Your teacher will make clear the parts you need.

Implementation

To implement your solution you need an adequate amount of test data. For example, in a database, data should be entered for at least 30 records. Each part of the software you have designed should be tested and evidence collected through printouts, reports and screen dumps for your write-up. The test strategy outlined in your design stage should be completed.

- Show the use of the software packages and document some of the features used. ☐

- State how the solution works and use diagrams to illustrate this. ☐

- Ensure the results you produce match the design stage. ☐

- Produce documentation for the user giving instructions on using the program, resource requirements and a troubleshooting guide. ☐

- Test your solution following the test strategy stated in the design section, and produce the evidence of testing. ☐

Evaluation

When you evaluate your project you should state whether the program met the objectives set. If possible, ask the person the program was written for to test the software and record their views. Be critical in your evaluation and, if an objective was not met, say why. State any shortcomings and possible future improvements.

- Compare the final solution with the design objectives set out in the analysis stage. ☐

- Test results from your solution may be given here or in the implementation stage. ☐

- Have your solution tested in situ doing the real task as set out in the analysis. ☐

- Document the opinions of other users testing and using your solution. ☐

- State the improvements made to the program as a result of testing. ☐

- State any enhancements and improvements that could be implemented. ☐

Testing

Testing requires a plan and the results should be documented to show it has been carried out logically. Data needs to be used to test a program. It should be:

- typical data that is expected by the program. The processing of this data can be compared to the original methods used to ensure that the program is processing the data correctly.

- data with known errors and extremes of data (eg very large and small numbers). This can be entered to see how the program copes. Validation checks in your program are important to stop this data being accepted ㉝.

All the functions and features built into the program need to be tested in a methodical manner.

Documentation

Computer software is often supplied with two types of documentation:

- **User manual** (or user documentation) containing the information for:
  - loading and running the program
  - using the different features of the program such as entering data, saving, editing, sorting and printing
  - troubleshooting when things do not work as they should.

  Extra marks can be obtained in your coursework for producing a small user manual to go with your software. Remember, it is for your intended user and should be written in plain English without any technical terms.

- **Technical manual** (or technical documentation) containing the technical details of the program together with data flow diagrams (see below) and flow charts to assist in making changes. Programs may need to be improved or updated. For example, many business programs had to be altered to cater for the date change in the year 2000. The original developers may not be available so this documentation, written in technical terms, is important.

Note: It is not necessary to write a separate technical manual for your school coursework; your project write-up should contain all the necessary information.

Data flow diagrams

These symbol diagrams show how the flow of data takes place during an operation. They are useful illustrations to include in the analysis stage of your ICT coursework.

Symbol	Description	Example	Symbol	Description	Example
	Data source or destination. Usually people or departments that supply or receive data.	Customer		Data store. Represents any storage: disk, magnetic tape, paper, filing cabinets, etc.	Master file
	Process. An operation that is performed on the data, eg calculations, sorting or printing.	Print customer details	→	Data flow. Shows the movement of data. The arrows should always be labelled.	Member's details, name and address →

Example: A customer sends off an order to a mail order company for goods. The company checks the order and payment when it arrives and then passes the order for processing. A 'picking list' is printed for the warehouse where the goods are packed and despatched to the customer. Details of the order are recorded in a 'Customer file' and an invoice is despatched. The stock levels in the stock file are adjusted as the order is being processed.

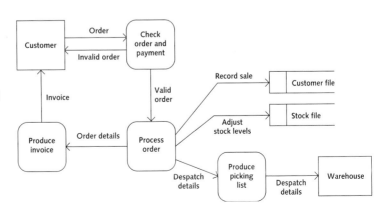

Software

- Software is the name given to computer programs.
- Important software programs include:

Program (example software)	Example uses	Key features
Database (Microsoft® Access, Information Workshop, Pinpoint)	To store, sort, search and retrieve information, eg details of customers, telephone directories, product details.	A database consists of records. In each record there are fields. Fields can be of different types, eg text, number, date, etc. Queries are used to search the records. Reports print out information from the database.
Word processor (Microsoft® Word, Write and Works, Word Perfect)	Writing letters, reports, projects, books, memos, essays.	Can edit, cut and paste, format text, spell-check, mailmerge.
Desktop publishing (Microsoft® Publisher, InDesign, Quark)	Leaflets, brochures, posters, advertisements, magazines, newspapers.	Frames, formatting, styles, import of text and graphics, layering, manipulation of images (rotation, reflection, cropping, shearing, resizing, etc).
Computer art and design (Microsoft® Paint, Adobe® Photoshop and Illustrator, CorelDRAW, AutoCAD)	Drawing and painting pictures, designing graphics, technical engineering drawing.	Freehand drawing, predefined shapes, colour fills, image manipulation, brush selection, labelling, 3D, simulating and testing designs.
Presentation (Microsoft® PowerPoint)	Presentations, lectures, lessons, assemblies, talks.	Text and graphics on slide, animation and sound effects, automatic slide sequences.
Web site design (Microsoft® FrontPage, Macromedia Dreamweaver)	Creating Web pages and Web sites.	HTML code, Web page design, imported text and pictures, tables, linking pages, URLs, hyperlinks.
Spreadsheet (Microsoft® Excel, Lotus 1-2-3)	Working with numbers, calculations, forecasting, business accounts, mathematical models.	Cells (containing text, numbers or formulae), graphs and charts, rows, columns, copying (replication), cell formatting, 'What if …?'.
Modelling and simulation (Flight Simulators, Sims, Microsoft® Excel)	Games, science experiments, weather forecasting, economic, safety and environmental models.	Mathematical model made to simulate reality, alter inputs and monitor effects, rules to define the model, data input from sensors.
Data logging and control (Insite, Logo, BASIC Stamp)	Scientific experiments and research, collecting weather data, monitoring river levels, controlling machines and instruments.	Sensors to input data, analogue signals changed to digital, calibration of sensors, real-time processing, data collected over long and short intervals, feedback.

Programming

- Software is written using computer programming languages.
- In computer programming, a series of commands written to solve a problem is called an algorithm.
- The instructions in a computer program can also be represented by a program flow chart.

Operating systems

- The operating system communicates between the applications software, eg the word processor, and the hardware.
- Operating systems control and manage:
  - the input and output (i/o) of the data
  - the order in which jobs are processed by the CPU
  - the management of files and peripherals
  - the allocation of resources including the memory and the CPU time
  - the system security.
- Computers can run in real time (processing data immediately) or in batch processing (when all the data has been collected).

User interfaces

- Command line interfaces require the user to type in commands, eg copy a:\project1.doc c: .
- Windows has a graphical user interface (GUI) making the software easy to use.
- Graphical user interfaces use windows, icons, menus and pointers (controlled by the mouse, trackerball or touch pad).

Word processor
(eg Microsoft Word)

Database
(eg Microsoft Access)

Presentation
(eg Microsoft PowerPoint)

Spreadsheet
(eg Microsoft Excel)

Hardware

Web site design
(eg Microsoft FrontPage)

Desktop publishing
(eg Microsoft Publisher)

A GUI operating system (in this case Windows) sits between hardware and software

Data is stored and processed inside a computer in digital form, as 1s and 0s. This is how computers operate, the electricity is either flowing along a circuit board track or wire, or it is not. This means that when we enter (or input) data into a computer, it must be converted into a set of digital pulses (0s and 1s).

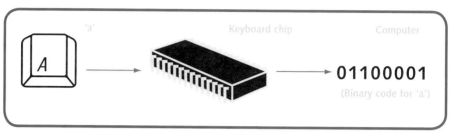

'a'   Keyboard chip   Computer

01100001

(Binary code for 'a')

Humans count in tens (decimal). Computers only use two digits, '0' and '1', so their number system is based on 2 (binary).

Each character on the keyboard has its own code made up of eight binary digits ⑨. The lower case letter 'a' shown has the code 01100001. Using eight binary digits enables 256 different codes to be formed, from 00000000 to 11111111. The binary codes allocated to the keyboard characters come from the **ASCII** (American Standard Code for Information Interchange) set and the same codes are used worldwide.

Inside the computer, the characters may be assigned different types of code from the ASCII set. This depends on the different processing taking place. For example, numbers are changed so arithmetic operations (add, subtract, multiply and divide) can take place. Different methods are used to code negative numbers and fractions.

Keyboard character	ASCII code							
0	0	0	1	1	0	0	0	0
1	0	0	1	1	0	0	0	1
2	0	0	1	1	0	0	1	0
A	0	1	0	0	0	0	0	1
B	0	1	0	0	0	0	1	0
C	0	1	0	0	0	0	1	1
a	0	1	1	0	0	0	0	1
b	0	1	1	0	0	0	1	0
c	0	1	1	0	0	0	1	1

Some ASCII codes

For example, the number 173 can be represented as:

ASCII

1   7   3

00110001   00110111   00110011

From the keyboard

Binary number

10110111

128	64	32	16	8	4	2	1
1	0	1	1	0	1	1	1

$128 + 32 + 16 + 4 + 2 + 1 = 173$

Inside the computer

Data and memory

When data is being used it is stored in the computer's RAM (random access memory), otherwise it can be stored as a file on a backing store, eg on the hard disk. Data can be compressed so that it takes up less space and compressed files take less time to send via the Internet. Popular software used to compress data is the WinZip program. The data must be decompressed before it can be used again.

Data files stored on disk are given a three-letter extension to identify the program that created the file. The table below shows four files created using different packages, each containing just the word 'Hello':

Program	File extension	Memory size	Memory size (zipped)*
Notepad file	.txt	5 Bytes	cannot reduce
Microsoft® Word	.doc	19 KB	1.7 KB
Microsoft® Paint	.bmp	1014 KB	1.8 KB
Microsoft® Excel	.xls	14 KB	1.7 KB

*Compressed using the WinZip program

Fixed and variable length records

Databases often have large data files. The records that hold the data can be of fixed or variable length as illustrated below:

Fixed length records

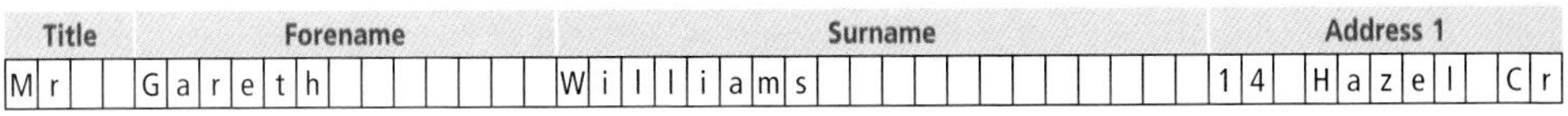

Title	Forename	Surname	Address 1
M r	G a r e t h	W i l l i a m s	1 4 H a z e l C r

Each field in the record is allocated a fixed number of bytes. Records can be located quickly as the position of the start of each record is known. A disadvantage of fixed length records is if the data is too long to fit into a field it must be abbreviated and if the data is shorter then memory is wasted.

Variable length records

Title	Forename	Surname	Address 1	Address 2
M r #	G a r e t h # W	i l l i a m s # 1 4	H a z e l C r e s c e n t # T e r l i n g	G r e

End of field markers

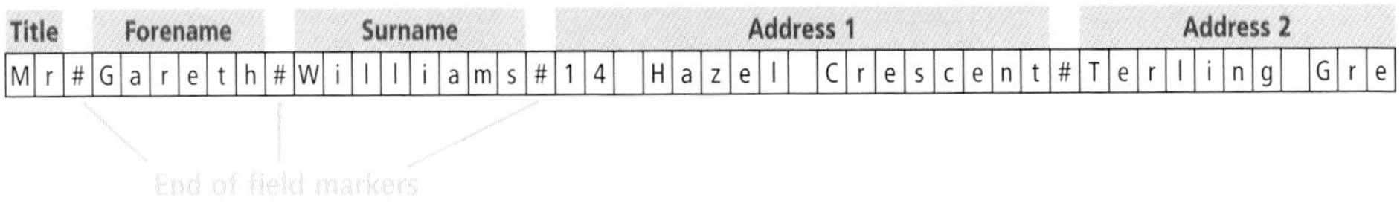

Here markers separate the fields and records and the field size is only as big as the data it contains. Little memory space is wasted but if a record, when edited, is increased in size it will not fit back onto the disk in the original position and this can lead to slower access times.

Calculating data size

When designing a database it is important to know how big the data file will become for the number of records the database will eventually hold. The table shows the fields in an address book database together with the allocated field sizes (fixed length fields).

Field name	Size (bytes/characters)
Title (Mr, Mrs, Prof, etc)	4
Initials	3
Surname	25
Address 1	25
Address 2	25
Address 3	20
Postcode	9
Telephone (area code)	6
Telephone (number)	7
Total bytes	**124**

Each record occupies 124 bytes of data. If this database eventually held 15 million records then the size of the data file would be:

$$124 \times 15\ 000\ 000 = 1\ 860\ 000\ 000 = 1.73\ GB$$

Calculation

$$1\ 860\ 000\ 000/1024 = 1\ 816\ 406\ KB$$
$$1\ 816\ 404/1024 = 1774\ MB$$
$$1774/1024 = 1.73\ GB$$

Calculating the record size in a similar way for your ICT coursework database project is a useful addition to the design section, although you may not have as many records as this example!

Field sizes in Microsoft® Access

For text fields, as in the example above, the user specifies how many characters are used. The number of bytes used by this and other fields are shown in the tables below:

Field	Size
Text	User defines (up to 255 bytes)
Memo	Variable (up to 65 535 bytes)
Date/time	8 bytes
Currency	8 bytes
Auto number	4 bytes
Yes/No	1 bit (1/8th byte)
OLE object	File size of the object selected

Number fields	Size
Byte	1 byte
Integer	2 bytes
Long integer	4 bytes
Single	4 bytes
Double	8 bytes
Decimal	12 bytes

Data or information?

The words 'data' and 'information' often seem to mean the same thing. Characters stored in the computer are data but, if we know what those characters mean then it becomes information.

Example: We have the **data**:
02041952

What does it mean? Is it a product part number, a date, an account number or a telephone number? If we know it is a date, 2 April 1952, then it becomes information.

Information = Data + 'The context and structure of the data'

April 1952

M	T	W	T	F	S	S
	1	②	3	4	5	6
7	8	9	10	11	12	13
14	15	16	17	18	19	20
21	22	23	24	25	26	27
28	29	30				

Coding data

It is often useful to code the data in database fields ⑫. For example, if we were entering the subjects studied at school into a database field, we could code these as:

MA = Mathematics   EN = English   DT = Design and Technology

FR = French   PS = Psychology   PE = Physical Education

Advantages of coding data include:

- data is easier and quicker to enter
- less typing is required
- you are less likely to make spelling mistakes
- it uses less computer memory.

Database of singers			
Name:	Orbison Caruso		
Sex:	M	**Age**	22
Nationality:	US	**Voice:**	T
Repertoire:	C	**Languages:**	EN
	J		IT
	P		GE

Male
United States
Classical
Jazz
Pop
Tenor
English
Italian
German

An example of coding data

Because computers are very flexible machines and are used for a wide range of tasks, there are also many different input devices that have been designed. Effective input devices should capture data quickly and accurately. The accuracy of data input is very important. There is an old computer saying 'Garbage In, Garbage Out' (GIGO) – in other words, entering incorrect data will produce the wrong outputs. There are checks that the computer can perform on the incoming data ③③▸, but it is important to choose the input device that will collect the data most accurately.

Features of some input devices

The list below summarises some of the important features for a selection of input devices:

- **OMR (optical mark reader)** – Used for checking registers in schools, selecting numbers on lottery tickets and marking multiple-choice examination papers. An important input device because the marks made directly by people, using a pen or pencil, can be read at high speed into the computer. OMR can have a high rejection rate if the marks are not positioned accurately.

- **OCR (optical character recognition)** – Used for scanning documents into a word processor, reading from 'turnaround' documents (see below) and postcodes on letters. Here people and computers read the same data. Accurate input with printed characters but not handwriting.

- **Bar codes** – Used for code numbers on food items and books. Excellent input device for packaging, cheap to print, can be read upside-down and on curved packaging. Fast data capture. Accurate due to the use of check digits ③③▸.

- **MICR (magnetic ink character recognition)** – Quite a specialist input method only used on bank cheques. Special printers are required to print the magnetic ink characters. Fast, very accurate data entry; the magnetic particles are unaffected by users writing over the characters.

- **Magnetic stripe** – Found on plastic cards. Used on bank and library cards, for security access systems and in schools for attendance swipe cards. Fast and accurate data input. Only holds a limited amount of data and prone to copying (card fraud). Being replaced by integrated chip cards (ICCs) ④④▸.

- **Sensors** – Electronic devices designed to monitor the environment, eg heat, light, sound, pressure, acidity, etc. Able to provide large quantities of data continuously. Additional electronics are needed to convert analogue signals to digital. Need to be calibrated to give accurate readings.

- **Keyboard** – The most common input device available with computers (but not embedded computers or some PDAs). One of the slowest input devices and not very accurate as it is subject to typing errors.

Turnaround documents

These are documents output from the computer, then used to record additional information before being input back into the computer. They are useful for payment requests sent out by post, eg credit card, electricity and gas bills. The payment slip is pre-printed with the customer's details. When the slip and the payment are received, details of the payment are printed on the form and input back to the computer for processing.

Questionnaires (data capture forms)

Using a questionnaire is a popular method of capturing data for a database. You could use a questionnaire to obtain data from other students in school or to record the results from interviews. Colleges can use questionnaires to gather information about new students and businesses can use them to collect information from customers. You could use a questionnaire in the analysis section of your ICT coursework.

Designing questionnaires

Questionnaires need to be carefully thought out and well designed so that all the information needed is requested on the sheet. Where possible, make the data easy to enter by providing tick boxes and ensure that there is enough room for details and answers to be written in. Set out the questions to match the layout of the fields on the screen so that the data is easy to enter. Include help and notes to aid the completion of the questionnaire.

Boat sales

Type of boat	☐ SA (Sail)	☐ MO (Motor)
	☐ MS (Motor sailer)	☐ DI (Dinghy)

Make ▢▢▢▢▢▢▢▢▢▢▢▢▢▢

Construction	☐ Wood	☐ GRP	☐ Steel

Length (m) ▢▢▢ . ▢▢

Year built ▢▢▢▢

Price (£) ▢▢▢▢▢▢

Telephone ▢▢▢▢▢ – ▢▢▢▢▢▢

Date ▢▢ – ▢▢ – ▢▢

Description ▢▢▢▢▢▢▢▢▢▢▢▢

Key to disk

Key to disk is an input method where computer operators enter data at a keyboard and it is saved directly to magnetic disk. The process is associated with large companies where substantial amounts of data need to be entered before processing can begin (batch processing ㉕▶). As processing power increases, key to disk operations are becoming less important.

Output data

There are fewer output devices than there are input devices. Apart from computer control, the two main output devices are the printer and monitor (or projection system). When designing the output it is important to consider the target audience. Designing a presentation for a business meeting will be quite different to one prepared for primary school children.

Consider the level of technical data your audience will understand. For example, presenting a weather forecast synoptic chart will only be understood by an audience with a knowledge of meteorology. Be clear about the message that you mean to convey and, where appropriate, make use of diagrams, clip art, graphs, animation, sound, etc.

When producing a report from a database, be selective in the fields you choose to display ⑬▶.

Verification and validation are two checking processes applied to data being input to a computer to remove errors.

Verification

Verification is used to check that data is entered correctly. When people are entering data via a keyboard, mistakes can occur. Copying handwriting is called transcribing. Errors can result from spelling mistakes, reading poor handwriting, transposing numbers (changing numbers around) and entering data into the wrong row or column.

Several forms of verification are in current use. When you change your password on the computer network, you are requested to enter the new password twice. Typing it the second time is verifying your first entry. Another form of verification is when you order goods by using a catalogue number in a shop like Argos or MFI, or order by phone or over the Internet. The number is passed to the computer database and the description of the goods is returned and displayed on the screen or read to you by the sales assistant. Checking these details against what you ordered is a form of verification.

User name

garethw

Enter old password

****

Enter new password

****

Repeat new password

****

You can apply verification checks to your ICT coursework by proofreading, from the screen or a printout, the data you have entered with the original data on the data capture forms.

One common error that occurs when entering data is transposing numbers, for example, the number **254896** is entered as **254986**.

Validation

The computer carries out a validation check when the data is entered. The majority of these checks are designed and put in place by the person writing the software. For example, if you are designing your ICT coursework using a spreadsheet or database then you should include validation checks in the software to trap errors made when entering data.

When validation rules are set, a validation message can be entered which will appear on the screen if an incorrect value is entered. This message should explain the form of the data required.

One example of a validation check built into the computer is the spell-check function. As text is entered, the spell-check compares each word typed against words in the computer dictionary and will underline the word with a red line if it is not found. With autocorrect on, many misspelt words will be corrected automatically. Try typing 'teh' in Microsoft® Word to see if it corrects it to 'the'. Other types of validation check are listed on the page opposite.

- **Presence check** – A field in a database or cell of a spreadsheet can be set so that it cannot be left empty.

- **Character count** – The number of characters to be entered can be set. This can be between a minimum and maximum number or set to an exact number. For example, the position of a landmark on a map can be pinpointed by a six-figure map reference. The computer will display an error if there are more or fewer than six numbers in the map reference field.

G W I 0 9 P

- **Range check** – The data entered must be within the range specified. For example, the year group in a secondary school would be between Year 7 and 13. The range check applied is: $x > 6$ AND $x < 14$.

- **Picture check** – For each character entered it is specified as 'text' or a 'number'. For example, National Insurance numbers always have a similar structure of two letters, six numbers then one letter.

- **Cross field check** – When data is entered in one field, a check is made with another field to ensure that the data is consistent. For example, if the data entered into the gender field is 'M' for male then this would be inconsistent with the data 'Mrs' entered in the title field.

- **Table lookup** – The data entered is checked against values in a table to see if it is acceptable. For example, the illustration below shows products in a table. Any product code entered that is not in the table is invalid and an error generated.

Product number

2814

Error message!

Product number	Product description
2812	12 cm plant pot (brown)
2815	15 cm plant pot (brown)
2830	30 cm rectangular seed tray (green)
- - - -	

- **Hash total (control total)** – This check is used with moving or transmitting groups of numbers. The numbers in the batch are added together and the total attached to the end of the list of numbers. When the numbers arrive at their destination, they are added again and the total compared with the last number. If the numbers are different then the numbers have been corrupted during the move.

- **Check digit** – Numbers like product code numbers on food items, book numbers (ie ISBN) and bank account numbers are given check digits. Because these numbers are long they are more likely to be entered incorrectly. To add the check digit, a mathematical calculation is performed on the original number producing a single digit which is added to the end. When the number is entered into the computer, a similar calculation is performed. If a different check digit is generated then the number has not been entered correctly.

The method of generating check digits for the ISBN (International Standard Book Number) of this book uses the UPC (universal product code) method:

Stage 1: Multiply each digit in the number by a factor, which alternates between 1 for the odd digits and 3 for the even digits.

9	7	8	1	8	5	7	4	9	8	7	4
x1	x3	x1	x3	x1	x3	x1	x3	x1	x3	x1	x3
9	21	8	3	8	15	7	12	9	24	7	12 = 135

Stage 2: Add the products together.

Stage 3: Divide the total by 10.

$$135 / 10 = 13 \text{ remainder } 5$$

Stage 4: Subtract the remainder from 10 to get the check digit* $10 - 5 = 5$.

* There is one special case; if the remainder is '0' then the check digit is '0'. If you look at the ISBN for this book (on the second page or the back cover), you will see that the check digit calculated (ie 5) agrees with the one shown. This method traps 99% of common errors, such as getting two digits transposed (mixed up).

Master file

A master file contains all the data required for a job. For example, a business may have a data file containing all the details for paying manual wages. This would be the payroll master file.

> Payroll master file contains: Employee payroll number, name, address, tax code, bank sort code, bank account number, bank account name, hourly rate of pay, overtime rate of pay, total pay in tax year, total income tax paid in tax year, total pension paid in tax year and the total NI contribution paid.

Transaction file

A transaction file is a collection of records with data that is used to update the master file. Transaction files are used in batch processes where the data is collected together first before the program is run (25). In the payroll example, this would contain the hours worked during the month and any overtime payments.

> Payroll transaction file contains: Employee payroll number, hours worked, overtime hours worked.

Sorting the transaction file

In the payroll master file, the records are stored in order of employee number. When the merge with the transaction file takes place, the records for an employee must be found in each file before the calculations and updating can take place. By sorting the records in the transaction file into the same order as the records on the master file, the merging process is very efficient.

Generations of files

The three most recent versions of master files are called 'grandfather, father and son' files. When the batch file process is started (eg the payroll program run), the current master file becomes the 'father' and the new master file, created by merging the transaction file, becomes the 'son'.

A month later when the payroll program is run again, the 'father' becomes the 'grandfather', the 'son' becomes the 'father', ie the current master file, and the merge with the transaction file creates a new 'son' file.

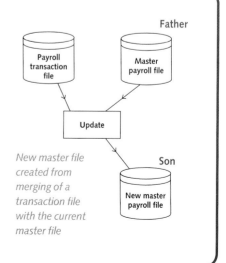

New master file created from merging of a transaction file with the current master file

System flow charts

System flow charts are used to show how data in a computer system is processed. It does not involve the complex detail of the program instructions (which are represented by the program flow chart (24▶) but it is a broad view of the system operation.

Symbol	Description	Example	Symbol	Description	Example
[rectangle]	**Process*** Represents a series of instructions to perform an operation.	Update files	Small document [doc symbol] Large document [doc symbol]	**Document** Symbol for a printed document output from the system.	Payslips
[diamond]	**Sort** Sort data or records in a file.	Sort records	[circle]	**Magnetic tape** Data stored on magnetic tape.	Back-up customer records
[disk symbol]	**Disk file** Data file stored on magnetic disk.	Master file	[keyboard symbol]	**Keyboard** Manual input through the keyboard.	

* This box could represent a whole program flow chart.

Example of a system flow chart

- Details of the hours worked and overtime done are entered for each employee.
- The data entered is validated and sorted into employee number order before being saved to a payroll transaction file.
- The payroll transaction file is merged with the master file and the updated details are stored in a new master file.
- Details in the master file, such as total tax paid, require updating each month. Reports and payslips are printed.

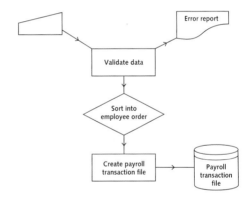

At the end of each month, the payroll program is run. The transaction file is **merged** with the master file. Each employee's wages, tax, pensions and NI contributions are calculated and their payslip printed. A file is created with details of the employees wages and bank account information to send to BACS (44▶) for payment through to their banks. Finally, the new master file is created with updated totals.

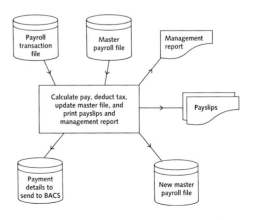

The data held on a computer is often much more valuable than the computer itself. In business, for example, computers are used to hold data on customers, sales, stock and finances and to lose this would be very serious.

Network security

When computers are used on a network, the network manager can add security to the data. Programs and data files can be allocated to specific users only. Programs can be allocated to only run on particular workstations and users must use passwords to gain access to the network. In addition, computers should be kept in locked rooms and notebooks secured in lockable cabinets.

Users can be allocated security permissions to files and programs on the network: No access; R – Read; W – Write; X – Execute; D – Delete. A user with RX access to a file/program can read it and run it but not write or delete it.

The most secure passwords are made from a mixture of uppercase letters, lowercase letters and numbers, for example: **eleNa4Temp**.

Passwords and encrypting data

Many files including Microsoft® Word, Excel and Access files can be made more secure by adding a password. Take care if you use this feature, you will not be able to open the file if you forget the password! Some companies use encryption software to prevent stolen data from being read.

Hackers

A hacker breaks encryption and passwords to gain unauthorised entry to computer systems. Some hackers can do an enormous amount of damage. They can change important data or add text and images that might damage a company's reputation. Computers that are accessible over networks are at most risk from hackers. Not all hackers cause harm; ethical hackers help to highlight gaps in security and alert organisations to possible security risks.

Computer viruses

A computer virus is a small program that is transmitted across a network or passed to the computer on disk. There are thousands of different viruses and more are being created every week by people intent on damaging other people's computer systems. Most viruses are now transmitted across the Internet, often as email attachments. Some spread very rapidly because when they infect a computer they are programmed to transmit themselves to all the users in that person's email address book. Good anti-virus software will protect a computer well but new viruses still cause millions of pounds worth of damage.

At the beginning of 2005, there were over 65 000 virus signatures records held by anti-virus software.

Computer fraud

Computer fraud is when someone illegally uses computer data for their own advantage. It is a bigger problem than most people think, because it is sometimes difficult to prove and companies do not always report it, for fear of damaging their reputation. Because it is easy to make a change to data in a computer with people noticing, 'transaction log files' are used to continuously record every change that operators make.

Looking after computer data

Computer data is stored on flash drives, hard disks and CD-ROMs. In order to protect these devices and the data they hold, it is necessary to examine the ways they can be damaged; then ways of protecting the data can be determined. The causes of lost or damaged data include:

- hard disk drive failures
- theft of equipment
- fire and floods
- hurricanes and earthquakes
- mistakes by users
- hacking attacks
- deliberate damage by users
- computer fraud
- computer viruses.

The best way to keep data safe is to make a back-up of the data every day and store it away safely.

Back-ups

To take a back-up means to take a copy of the data. This is essential in business and all organisations where there is a reliance on computers. In many situations, computers are connected by a local area network ⟨37⟩ and the data from all workstations is stored on the network server. When the back-up is run, usually during the night, the data from all users on the network is copied. If a back-up is taken at the end of each day, then the most that can be lost is one day's work. Often, special tape streamer units ⟨8⟩ are used which save the data on to magnetic tape cassettes. These cassette tapes can typically hold up to 400 GB of data allowing all the data on the server's hard drives to be backed up. A number of tapes should be used in rotation so that a back-up copy can always be kept away from the premises.

The tape containing the data must be stored in a safe place. If it is stored with the computer then a fire will destroy the original data **and** the back-up copies. The tapes should be placed in a fireproof safe or staff may be encouraged to take data tapes home with them.

Hard drive failure

Hard disk drives are physical devices with moving parts so they will eventually wear out. Failure of a hard disk on a network server could bring down all the services. The repair would mean calling an engineer to replace the drive unit and then reinstalling all the data from the back-up tape – at least half a day of down time. For some businesses **no** down time is acceptable so alternative methods are used. RAID (Redundant Array of Inexpensive Disks) systems allow the server to continue. There are different levels of RAID operation. One level uses two hard drives, one a mirror of the other which takes over if the first drive fails. Another level of RAID uses an array of disk drives, six or more.

Down time is when computers are not available for use due to hardware or software failure or maintenance.

Keeping data safe

Removable media such as CDs, DVDs and USB memory sticks must be treated with care. If they are carried around, make sure that they are not physically damaged. They should not be stored where it can get too hot, eg in direct sunlight. They should not be allowed to get damp or dirty. When labelling CDs and DVDs, only write on the top of the disc and use a felt-tip pen. Discs should be kept in their cases when not in use, as a scratched disc can become unreadable.

Data

- Data becomes information if we know its context and structure.
- Data is stored in the computer in a digital form of '0's and '1's.
- The '0' and the '1' are stored in memory called a 'bit' (binary digit).
- A keyboard character is coded using an ASCII code of eight bits and stored in a byte of memory.
- Data inside the computer may be coded differently, eg in binary for arithmetic operations.
- Files of data can be compressed, using programs like WinZip, to take up less memory.
- Compressed files must be decompressed before they can be processed.

Databases

- Database files consist of records of either fixed or variable length.
- File size can be estimated from the number of records multiplied by record length.
- For fixed length records, the length is the sum of the size of each field.
- Data can be coded:
  - to take up less memory
  - so it is quicker and easier to enter
  - to be less prone to spelling mistakes and errors.

Data capture

- Prior to the data being entered, it can be collected using questionnaires or data capture forms.
- The layout of data capture forms should match the input screens so that the data can be entered easily.
- Questionnaires should be designed so they can be completed quickly and easily.
- Data can be input to a computer through many different input devices.
- Each input device has been designed for a particular purpose, eg magnetic ink character recognition (MICR) for bank cheques and bar code readers for goods in shops.
- Validation checks are used so that the computer can check the incoming data for errors.
- Verification involves entering data twice and checking or proofreading to ensure better accuracy.

Data validation

- These are checks written into the program by the user and then carried out by the computer as the data is entered.

- Validation checks include presence checks, character counts, range checks, picture checks, cross field checks, table lookup, hash totals and check digits.

- The validation check(s) used will depend on what data is being entered (often only one check is applied to a data field).

Presenting data (data output)

- Data can be presented by displaying it on a monitor or as a hard copy printout from the printer.

- When designing the presentation of data you should consider the audience.

- Where appropriate, use tables, graphs, charts and illustrations to enhance the presentation.

- When creating a report from a database only select the fields that are required for the task.

File handling

- A master file contains all the data required for a job.
- A transaction file contains new data that is used to update the master file as a batch process.
- The transaction file is merged with the master file when the batch process is run.
- During the merge a new updated master file is produced.
- There are three generations of master files – grandfather, father and son.
- After a merge, the old master file becomes the father and the new master file, the son.
- Transactions files must be sorted before merging with the master file.
- System flow charts are used to illustrate file handling processes.

Security of data

- Removable media (eg USB memory sticks) need to be protected from physical damage, heat, water and dirt.
- Data files can be protected from unauthorised use by:
  - passwords and levels of access
  - restricting physical access to computer workstations, eg locked rooms
  - coding the data with encryption software.
- Data should be copied regularly by taking a back-up.
- Organisations and businesses with networks should back-up the data on the server every night.
- Daily back-ups are often made on magnetic tape but CD-RW discs and other hard drives can be used.

A single computer (or stand-alone computer) is a useful tool for work and leisure activities but when it is joined to other computers in a network it becomes much more powerful. Users can communicate across a network and share data and peripherals with other users.

There are two main types of network:

- **WAN** (wide area network) – Computers are connected together over a wide geographical area. For example, connecting to the Internet.
- **LAN** (local area network) – Computers are connected together on the same site. For example, in a school or an office.

Topology

There are three ways in which LAN workstations can be connected:

Star network:

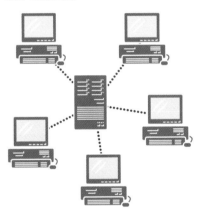

Bus network:

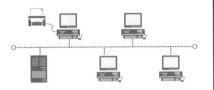

+ Easy and inexpensive to install, least amount of cable required.
− If the cable fails, all of the computers will be affected.
− Performance of the network slows down with more users.

Ring network:

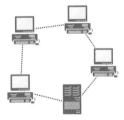

+ Performance of network is less affected by the number of computers in use.
+ Fast data speeds.
+ A cable failure does not affect other users.
− Uses more cable.

+ Data traffic faster than bus network as traffic flows in one direction only.
− Cable failure affects all of the workstations.

Bus and ring networks are still used but the star topology is the most common network configuration. The star topology has a greater fault tolerance than the other networks.

> **Topology** is the name given to the way in which computers are connected in the network. For example, we could say that workstations are connected in a star topology.

A server is a powerful computer which holds the operating system software to run the network. For example, Windows NT, Windows 2003 Server or Linux. Some of the tasks for this software include monitoring the network, creating users, handling printer spool queues and allowing access permissions to be set on files and folders. Some networks are set up so that the application software (Word, Excel, etc) is held on the server and passed to the user's workstation when required. On other networks, the programs are held on each workstation and only files are saved to the server.

On larger networks, there may be servers dedicated to particular tasks. For example:

- File servers – Store files and data.
- Print servers – Spool queues for the network printers.
- Mail servers – Receive, send and store emails.
- Internet servers – Store (cache) frequently-accessed Web pages and provide security against hackers and viruses.

A typical small network

The illustration below shows a client-server network, often found in schools and businesses. The server stores the programs, the users' data and printer (spool) queues.

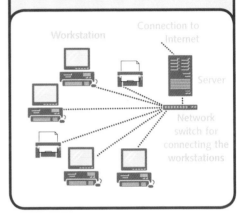

Advantages and disadvantages of networks

+ Users can access their data from any workstation.
+ Users can communicate with others across the network.
+ Data, including documents, files and database records, can be shared.
+ Programs can be shared from the file server to workstations.
+ Printers and expensive peripherals can be shared – workstations do not need their own printer.
+ Data is safer as it is stored centrally on the server, which can be copied onto back-up tapes each night.
+ There is greater security as the network administrator can assign access rights for programs to users and workstations.

– The cost of installation is greater.
– A network manager is often needed to run the system.
– If a server fails, a number of workstations may be affected.
– There is a greater threat from hackers and the spread of viruses (35).

This section looks at some of the ways in which computers can be connected when they are networked.

LAN (local area network)

- **Wire cables** – This is the most common means of connecting computers in a LAN. There are different types of cable but UTP (unshielded twisted pair) cable is popular. The cable contains eight insulated, colour-coded wires twisted together to form four pairs. This cable has a category rating (eg Cat 5) to ensure it meets the required standards.

  Twisted pair

  + Wire is cheap.
  − Limit to the length of cable (< 200 m).

- **Fibre-optic cable** – As the backbone of a network or where cables on the site need to travel outside underground or over roofs, fibre-optic cable is used. The computer data is carried on a beam of light that travels along the strand of glass.

  Thin glass fibre   A light beam travels through the fibre, carrying the digital signal

  Protective sheaths

  + High data speeds.
  + Free from electrical interference.
  + Does not suffer from corrosion.
  − Cables and installation costs are more than using UTP cables.

WAN (wide area network)

- **Telephone wires** – Much of the network traffic from homes and businesses to the Internet is done via copper telephone wires. The speed of data transmissions can be slow (with modems) but newer technology (ADSL) has increased transmission speeds considerably.

- **Fibre-optic cable** – Data can be transmitted over long distances and at high speeds. Fibre cables are laid underground along the central reservations of motorways to connect towns and cities.

- **Microwave** – It can be very expensive to lay cables through towns and microwave links are often more practical. Network data 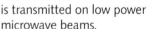 is transmitted on low power microwave beams.

  + Secure data communication between sites.
  + Cost-effective method of linking buildings in towns.
  − Direct line of sight required between the transmitting and receiving microwave dishes.

- **Satellite** – Network data is transmitted to an orbiting satellite which then relays the signal to a ground station hundreds of miles away.

  + Communication over large distances, across continents.
  − Costly to put satellites into orbit.

Connecting to a WAN (the Internet)

- **Dial-up modem** – The word 'modem' is short for **mo**dulator **dem**odulator. Modems convert the digital signals in the computer to analogue signals which can travel down a telephone line. They also convert incoming signals back into a digital form. A dial-up modem sends data by making a standard telephone call to the user's service provider, so the user is charged by the minute, as for a normal voice call. The maximum speed for a dial-up modem is 56 kbps (kilobits per second). This is too slow for most modern uses of the Internet, so dial-up modems have almost all been replaced by faster connection types.

- **ADSL (asymmetric digital subscriber line)** – ADSL uses the same telephone lines as the older dial-up systems, but transmits in a different frequency range using a different kind of modem. This means that it can provide much faster data speeds. From the customer to the Internet service provider (39)▶, data is sent at speeds of up to 640 kbps*. In the other direction, from the service provider to the customer, data rates can reach 8 Mbps* (8 million bits per second). These speeds enable users to download large files such as pictures, music and video clips quickly. Customers with ADSL access are connected to the Internet 24 hours a day for a fixed monthly charge.

- **Cable** – Some cable operators provide an Internet service over the same cables they use for television. A special cable modem is required, and the data transfer speeds are comparable to those achieved using ADSL (although speeds of 30 Mbps are possible in theory).

Engineer working on ADSL equipment at the Battersea Exchange, London

* Typical speeds are much slower

Network cards – To connect a computer to a local area network it must have a network card. This card slots into a socket on the motherboard and provides a socket at the back of the computer for the network cable.

Data transmission rate – This is measured in bits per second (bps). Remember, 8 bits are needed to store one character. 100 Mbps (100 million bits per second) is a normal transmission rate for network cables (approximately 10 000 characters per second). Giga bit devices, ten times faster, are becoming the standard.

Broadband

Broadband is the name given to any data communication channel that has a wide bandwidth and can carry a large quantity of data. Many UK schools are now connected to the Internet using a broadband connection with typical data speeds of 10 Mbps. This connection could be by:

- copper wire using ADSL connections (see above)
- fibre-optic cable
- microwave links.

The Internet is a huge international network made up of many smaller networks linked together like a spider's web. It was started in 1969 as a research project funded by the US military. By the end of that year, a total of four computers were linked to the network. Today, millions of computers are connected.

The Internet provides a vast range of information resources that can be accessed from your school or home computer. This information can be placed onto the Web by the millions of different users around the world without any form of regulation. This means that care must be taken when viewing different sites. Some material is very exact, detailed and informative; other sources may hold inaccurate information, and some sites hold quite offensive material.

Connecting to the Internet

To connect a computer to the Internet requires:

- **A physical connection** – Most users now have a broadband connection as ADSL ⑧.

- **Communications software or Web browser** – The most common browsers are Microsoft® Internet Explorer, which comes as part of the Microsoft® Windows operating system, and Mozilla Firefox. Most Macs use Safari.

- **A connection agreement with an Internet service provider (ISP)** – Depending on the service required, this may be free or involve a regular subscription payment.

Internet service providers (ISPs)

There are many organisations providing users with the link, or point of presence (PoP), to the Internet. The communication software on the computer (eg Internet Explorer) holds the dialling number for the ISP in the program options. Depending on the type of connection, a computer may be permanently connected to their ISP or will dial up over the phone line when the computer needs to access the Internet. ISPs allocate disk space to users for Web sites and provide email accounts. Some ISPs offer users free telephone call numbers for Internet access. Some major ISPs include BT Internet, Orange, Virgin and AOL.

World Wide Web

The World Wide Web is what draws most people onto the 'Net'. The Web allows people to publish multimedia pages, containing text, graphics, sound and video information for users of the Internet to view.

Organisations, businesses, schools and individuals can create their own Web pages using Web authoring software like FrontPage (from Microsoft) or Dreamweaver (from Macromedia) ⑲.

Different Web pages can be connected using hyperlinks; in other words, new pages are selected by clicking with the mouse on the linking text or graphics. Each Web page on the Internet has a unique address, starting with the letters http:// (standing for hypertext transfer protocol). These Web addresses are termed URLs (uniform resource locators). An example of a Web site address is http://www.pearsonpublishing.co.uk/.

Forums

Forums (or fora) are a form of electronic noticeboard, usually hosted on a Web site. When users visit the forum, they can read messages or leave their own for others to read. Most forums are dedicated to a particular theme such as football, cooking or books. People post messages either to provide or request information, or to give their opinions. Forums often have FAQ (frequently asked questions) sections which enable users to avoid asking questions that have already been answered many times before.

Web browsers

A Web browser is software for viewing the content of Web pages. It interprets the HTML code and displays text and graphics on the screen. There is a common standard for how this should be done. However, different Web browsers interpret the commands slightly differently, hence designers must plan and test their pages carefully to ensure that the end user sees what they are supposed to.

Extra features or interactivity can be added to Web pages using JavaScript, CGI scripts or plug-ins such as Macromedia Flash. These can make Web sites very dynamic and exciting, but not all users will be able to see the material.

As well as storing details of the pages visited in a 'History' folder, the parts that make up the Web pages are stored (or cached) on the hard disk of the computer. Retrieving data from a hard disk is faster than over an Internet connection so if a page is requested more than once, it is retrieved and displayed much more quickly.

Web browsers also allow you to download material from Web sites to your hard disk, eg software updates, graphics, video clips, games and much more. Copyright permission must be obtained before publishing or distributing any material that has been downloaded.

Interesting sites can be added to your favourites for quick access at a later date

History stores details of sites visited, grouped by days and weeks

Storing URL Web links to recently visited sites

Web address, also known as a URL – in this case the home page for Yahoo!

Links to other parts of the Web site

A Web browser – Internet Explorer

The Internet has changed the way people live. It is no longer necessary to leave our homes to shop. Food, clothes, in fact almost all goods can be purchased online and delivered to our doorsteps.

e-business

e-business, also known as e-commerce, is the name given to trading over the Internet. This might be between one business and another, for example a manufacturer ordering materials; this is called B2B (business to business). Or it might involve using the Internet to sell to consumers; this is called B2C (business to consumer). Selling goods over the Internet opens up new markets. Internet Web sites are accessible around the world and so all companies, both large and small, have equal opportunities to reach new international markets 24 hours a day, 365 days of the year.

Business use of the Internet

Companies make use of the Internet in varying ways. These can be categorised into four levels:

- **Level 1** – The Internet is just used to send email messages to staff, customers or suppliers.
- **Level 2** – Web sites are created where customers can view the products and read detailed descriptions of both the goods and the company. Customers can contact the company by email via the Web site.
- **Level 3** – Customers can place orders on the Web site and pay for the goods by credit cards over a secure (encrypted) link. Customers may be able to view whether the goods are in stock and track the progress of their order. The business may offer service and support over the Internet to the customer.
- **Level 4** – Orders placed by customers over the Internet start automated processes in the business. These might include ordering parts from suppliers, scheduling the time and date for making the goods, and reserving space on the delivery lorry. The customer's payment is also fully integrated into the company's account systems.

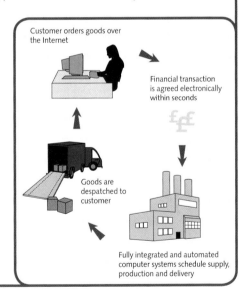

Customer orders goods over the Internet

Financial transaction is agreed electronically within seconds

Goods are despatched to customer

Fully integrated and automated computer systems schedule supply, production and delivery

Some Web sites receive more visits (hits) than others. The official Web site for the 2000 Olympic Games received six and a half billion hits over a ten-day period while the Games were in progress. This represents an average of 7500 hits per second, 24 hours a day.

Web site design

For businesses selling goods over the Internet, it is very important to have a well-designed Web site. If users experience frustrating delays while graphics download or find ordering goods complicated then they are likely to look elsewhere. A well-designed Web site should include the following features:

- Web pages that appear quickly (without delays as graphic images are loaded)
- professional-looking pages without spelling or grammatical errors
- instructions for first-time users
- a search facility where goods can be located using only part of the description
- a straightforward ordering process

- secure encryption techniques for payment of goods
- a page design that fits the user's screen
- marked out-of-stock products
- pictures, brief descriptions and reviews of the goods
- easy navigation and product location.

Because Web sites can be accessed from around the world, a further consideration is to offer a choice of languages to the user.

Researching information

In order to find Web pages containing material on a specific subject, a **search engine** can be used. This is a Web site which, when you type in a few words or phrases, can find Web pages whose content is in some way related. It will then present these as a list of hyperlinks, usually with a short description.

Ask.com home page – uk.ask.com

The Internet can provide resource material on almost any subject but it must be used with care. There is no guarantee that information contained in an Internet article is accurate. Look for documents from official Web sites, eg government or company sources; they are more likely to contain accurate facts than other people's opinions. When searching for information using search engines, think carefully about the key words you use, otherwise you may have thousands of article references returned.

Advantages and disadvantages of using the Internet for research include:

Advantages:
- + The Internet is readily available from most computers.
- + There is a huge amount of information available on most subjects.
- + Articles are updated daily.
- + Search engines are available to help find information on topics.
- + Information is available in multimedia form.
- + Email can be used to request further information.

Disadvantages:
- − It can be hard to decide whether the information you find is reliable.
- − It can be difficult to find the information you want from searches.

There are many ways of communicating with people and so we can choose which method to use depending on the nature of the communication. A hundred years ago the options were limited to 'posting a letter', later the telephone was invented and then the fax (facsimile) machine. It has only been in the last decade that mobile phones, text messaging and personal emails have become commonplace. The table opposite compares these different methods of communication.

Email

Email, or electronic mail, is a way of sending messages and computer files across the Internet. When you join the Internet, your Internet service provider (ISP) ⊙39► provides you with an email address, eg info@pearson.co.uk. Your school may also issue you with an address, and organisations like Microsoft® Hotmail offer free email accounts (see below).

Email allows messages to be sent to anyone on the Internet, even on the other side of the world – often for the price of a local telephone call.

Receiving an email

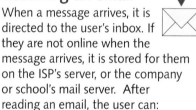

When a message arrives, it is directed to the user's inbox. If they are not online when the message arrives, it is stored for them on the ISP's server, or the company or school's mail server. After reading an email, the user can:

- delete the message
- file the message by storing it on disk
- send back a reply
- forward the message to one or more other people.

Sending an email

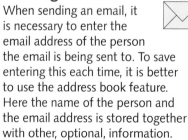

When sending an email, it is necessary to enter the email address of the person the email is being sent to. To save entering this each time, it is better to use the address book feature. Here the name of the person and the email address is stored together with other, optional, information.

Another feature of the address book is that people can be assigned to a group. If the group name is selected in the 'To' line of the email it will be sent to all the members of the group.

Web-based email

Many companies such as Microsoft® Hotmail, Yahoo! and Google's Gmail offer free email accounts that are accessed entirely via a Web site, rather than the emails being stored on your computer as they are with most ISP accounts. This means that people who do not have an Internet connection at home or at work can still use email. Many of these now offer several gigabytes of storage for emails and attached files.

Attached files

Files can be attached to emails and sent to other users. These can be word processor documents, spreadsheets, database files or graphic images. This is a fast and efficient method of transferring data, but care must be taken when receiving attachments from unknown sources as viruses can be transmitted in this way.

	What is required?	Advantages	Disadvantages
Post	Envelope, paper and stamp	• Easy to do • No expensive equipment • Send/receive hard copy	• Slow (days) • Stamp more expensive than digital transmissions
Telephone	Telephone and socket or mobile phone	• Instant communication • Leave messages	• No hard copy of message • Calls and line rental expensive (on mobiles)
Text message	Mobile phone	• Instant communication if receiver's phone on • Messages stored • Less expensive than a phone call	• Only short messages are practical • Difficult to type message
Fax	Fax machine (or computer) and socket	• Instant transmission of documents	• Receiver must have fax machine • Usually only black and white
Email	Computer	• Quick to send • Inexpensive • Can attach documents	• Can transmit computer virus
Video conferencing	Computer, camera, microphone, broadband WAN connection	• Interactive image and voice communication	• Expensive equipment • Receiver also needs similar equipment

Spam and unsolicited mail

Spam is the name given to unsolicited emails that are sent out in large quantities to users on the Internet. Unsolicited mail is mail that has not been requested by the user. Spammers, the people that send spam emails, may send thousands of Internet users the same message. The contents of spam emails include 'get-rich-quick' schemes, chain mail, pyramid schemes, miracle health cures, loan and credit schemes and pornographic material. Spam is a nuisance as it clogs up the Internet, slowing down the network for genuine users and it takes time to remove spam email from mailboxes each day.

Email security

The content of an email message is not necessarily private – it can be read by others during its journey across the Internet. Some authorities scan emails to see if they contain certain words and channel them off for viewing if they do. There is software available, for example, PGP (Pretty Good Privacy), which encrypts email messages before you send them. Some governments ban encryption because it stops them from monitoring email traffic.

When you receive an email, particularly in business, you need to be sure that it is from the person it says it is. It is possible to use a digital signature, where additional data is added to an email to verify that it comes from that person.

Mobile phones and video conferencing

Mobile phones

Some mobile phones can receive Internet pages and email messages. These are called WAP (wireless application protocol) phones and have colour screens to display the data. To receive Internet Web pages on mobile phones, the existing HTML code ⟨19⟩ needs to be rewritten in WML (wireless markup language).

Applications

WAP phones receive cut-down versions of Internet pages and are used to check:

- bank balances
- share prices
- train times, delays and cancellations
- traffic information and delays
- news and weather
- sports news and results.

And to:

- order foreign currency
- pay bills
- transfer money
- buy travel tickets (rail and air).

A hotel chain with 56 hotels across the country has launched a WAP service that allows customers to use their mobile phones to check if a room is available at one of the hotels, to make a reservation and to receive travel directions.

Development of mobile phones

WAP phones are in constant development and are evolving through different 'generations' or G, including:

- **2 G** – Capable of sending and receiving short text messages. Uses Global System for Mobile communication (GSM) at 9.6 Kbps. This is very slow when compared with a home connection to the Internet.

- **2.5 G** – Uses General Packet Radio Service (GPRS) at 115 Kbps. With these mobiles, the Internet connection is always on.

- **3 G** – This uses Universal Mobile Telecommunications System (UMTS) with data rates of 2 Mbps. It provides full colour and video images.

In 2000, the UK Government raised £22.5 billion by auctioning off the licences for 3 G phones to five companies.

Video conferencing

Video conferencing means talking to another person across a network while watching the person on live video via a camera. The simplest form of video conferencing can be set up at home using a Web cam, microphone and conferencing software.

Installations

The equipment needed for video conferencing depends on the size of the group involved:

- For individuals, small desktop arrangements are suitable with fixed focus cameras.
- For groups of two to seven users, larger display monitors are required and cameras may have pan, tilt and zoom functions. When catering for groups of this size the equipment is often mounted on a trolley to make it mobile.
- For groups of eight or more, several microphones (possibly voice activated), a projection display and a camera with swivel and zoom facilities may be needed. For these larger groups, equipment may be permanently installed in a dedicated room.

To transmit live video it is important to have fast network data speeds; for a wide area network, broadband connections are required. Sometimes a card is fitted inside the computer, called a **codec card**, which compresses the data before it is transmitted and decompresses incoming data.

Benefits of video conferencing

In business, meetings can take place between staff from different offices without the need for time and the expense in travelling. In schools, it can be used to help learn foreign languages by conferencing with schools abroad or even deliver specialist courses where teachers are not available in the school. In primary schools, pupils can find out more about school life at a secondary school by video conferencing with older students.

Networks

- Two or more computers connected together form a **network**.
- Computers connected together on the same site form a local area network (**LAN**).
- Computers connected over a wide geographical area form a wide area network (**WAN**), eg the Internet.
- **Advantages** of networks include:
  - can access files from any station
  - share resources, eg programs, data files and expensive peripherals (eg printers, plotters)
  - can communicate with other users
  - better security of data (ie passwords, access rights, central storage of data for back-ups).
- **Disadvantages** of networks include:
  - more expensive, may need a network manager
  - many stations affected if server fails
  - easier for system to be attacked by hackers or virus programs.
- Servers use special operating systems, eg Windows 2003 Server, to manage network tasks.

Network topology

- Network topology describes the way computers are connected.
- There are three types of network topology; the star, ring and bus.
- Star topology networks have the best fault tolerance.

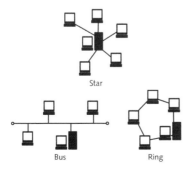

Star

Bus

Ring

Internet

- Connecting a computer to the Internet requires a modem (or similar), Web browser and ISP.
- Web browsers can store the Internet links (URLs) to sites with 'shortcuts', 'history' and 'favorites'.
- Web pages are stored (cached) on the hard drive for faster access if requested again.
- Features of the Internet include: email, forums, chat rooms, advertising, distribution of software, customer support, e-business and online booking.
- Uses of the Internet include:
  - doing business (eg purchasing goods, e-business or e-commerce)
  - researching information
  - sending and receiving email.
- **Advantages** of using the Internet for research include:
  - a huge amount of up-to-date information is available
  - use of search engines to find material quickly
  - sound, graphics, video and animation help to explain material.
- **Disadvantages** of using the Internet for research include:
  - there is so much information it can be hard to find what you need
  - anyone can post information, so you need to make sure your source is reliable.

Email

- Email allows users to send messages and file attachments to other users on the Internet.

- Features of email include: reply, forward, address book, mailing lists, folders, attachments and printing.

- Your email account may be provided by an ISP, your school or workplace, or a Web-based email service.

Mobile phones and video conferencing

- **Mobile phones** can connect to the Internet using WAP (wireless application protocol).

- Common uses include checking train times and traffic information, paying bills and reading news, weather and sports results.

- **Video conferencing** means talking to another person across a network while watching them via a camera.

- A Web cam, microphone and appropriate software are required for video conferencing.

Connections

- LAN computers are connected by cables (UTP and fibre-optic) and wireless.
- WAN computers are connected by copper telephone cables, fibre-optic cables, microwave links and satellites.
- Computers require a network interface card to connect them to a LAN.
- Almost all Internet users now have a broadband connection. This uses a wide range of frequencies to transmit large amounts of data quickly. An ADSL connection running at 2 Mbps would take just over a minute to download a 20 MB file.
- Data transfer rates around local area networks are faster still, as shown in the table below:

	Typical data speed	Approximate time to transfer a 20 MB file
Wireless*	54 Mbps	3 seconds (for one computer)
UTP (unsheilded twisted pair) cable	100 Mbps	1.6 seconds
Fibre-optic cable	1000 Mbps	0.16 seconds

*For wireless networks, the 54 Mbps is shared between the number of workstations

The use of computers is vital in banks. They are used to keep records of bank customers, calculate interest, process cheques, transfer money between accounts, handle credit and debit cards and operate cash machines!

Cash machines

ATM (automatic teller machine) is the proper name for the cash machine or dispenser. All ATMs are connected by a wide area network to the bank's computers. When you insert your card and enter your **PIN (personal identification number)**, it is checked against the customer details on the chip in the card. The cash you withdraw is deducted immediately from your account.

To obtain cash from the machine:

1   Insert the card in the slot.
2   Enter the PIN (personal identification number).
3   Choose the service required (cash, check balance, request statement, etc).
4   Select the amount of cash required.
5   Take back the card.
6   Take the money.
7   Take the receipt (if requested).

(When these machines were first installed, points 5 and 6 in the procedure above were reversed. This led to people forgetting to take their cards.)

There are more than 25 000 ATMs in the UK. Each machine is expensive to manufacture as it needs to incorporate a small safe to hold the money and have very precise mechanisms to ensure the exact amount of cash is dispensed. Machines are built securely into walls with access to the rear for restocking with money and connecting via a network to the bank.

Obtaining cash at any time of the day or night from an ATM is often more convenient than visiting the bank or building society. Also, employers have moved away from paying their workers in cash. Instead, they transfer funds directly to the employees' bank accounts, so the need for ATMs has grown.

Automated payments

Many payments are set up to run automatically by linking the banks' computers to the **Bankers' Automated Clearing Service (BACS)** computer centre in London – the largest automated clearing house in the world. These automated payments fall into two types:

- **Credits** – Paying money into our accounts, including wages, salaries and pensions.
- **Debits** – Paying money from our accounts (direct debits), including subscriptions, household bills (eg gas, electricity, oil, water rates, council tax), rent, insurance premiums, loan repayments.

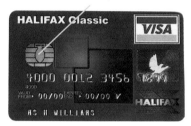

A tiny integrated circuit chip is embedded into the card. The silicon chip contains a processor and memory. Conductive pads on the card enable data to be input to and output from the chip

Plastic bank cards have a small chip built into them that holds encrypted data about a customer's account. When the card is placed into a card reader or ATM, this data is read and transferred to the computer. There are various types of plastic card:

- **Cash card** – This can only be used to withdraw money from an ATM.
- **Debit card** – Money is taken directly from your bank account electronically.

- **Credit card** – Unlike a debit card, money is not taken out of your account straight away; you receive a bill at the end of each month. Paying by credit card for goods over the Internet or by phone is safer than using a debit card.

Plastic cards are a convenient and safe way to pay for goods, reducing the need to carry large amounts of cash around. They are often used to pay for the weekly food shop, fuel, clothes and goods purchased over the Internet.

Security

Banks have recently changed to **integrated chip cards (ICCs)** (or **'smart cards'**) because they are more secure than using magnetic stripes alone. Customers now use their PIN in shops instead of a signature, and the data is harder for criminals to copy or change. Cards still have the magnetic stripe as a back-up.

Cheques

Each day in the UK, millions of cheques are cashed. When a cheque is passed to the bank for payment, the amount the cheque has been made out for is printed on the bottom of the cheque, alongside three other groups of numbers. The ink used in this process contains tiny magnetic particles so that the characters can be read and input to a computer. The cheque is then passed for 'clearing', where the four groups of numbers are read. Using a recording head similar to that on a tape recorder, the numbers can be read at great speed (3000 cheques per minute). This input method is known as **magnetic ink character recognition (MICR)** 4 ▶.

Characters written in magnetic ink

Electronic funds transfer (EFT)

When a card is used to obtain cash from an ATM, data is transmitted electronically to the bank and the equivalent amount of money is electronically removed from the user's account. When paying for shopping in a supermarket using 'plastic' such as a Switch card, the payment is transferred electronically from the customer's account to the shop's account. This electronic movement of money is known as an electronic funds transfer (EFT) 45 ▶.

Computers are used by supermarkets to process goods at the checkout, keep the correct quantities of stock in the store, order new goods, process information on loyalty cards and operate Internet shopping. In the supermarket, the computerised checkout tills are connected to back office computers forming a local area network. There are also links from the store to suppliers and banks, forming a wide area network 38▶.

Checkout tills

Checkout tills are central to the computerisation of the supermarket. At the checkout, the laser scans the bar code on the product and passes the bar code number to the central database where details of all the stock are held. The database program returns the price and description of the product to the till. An itemised receipt is then generated. If the customer pays for the goods using a credit or a debit card, the till communicates with the bank over the wide area network to process the transaction. As each product is scanned and sold, the stock levels are adjusted.

Stock control – Computers control the amount of goods a store has

Bar code is scanned into the computer

Loyalty card – Encourage customers to return by awarding points, gifts and vouchers

Credit card – The electronic bill connects by networks to transfer money from bank accounts

Electronic funds transfer point of sale (EFTPOS)

The movement of money electronically over a network is called electronic funds transfer (EFT). In a supermarket, the checkout tills are the point where the sale takes place – this is called point of sale (POS). As these tills are connected via a local area network to a wide area network and can handle 'card' payments, they become electronic funds transfer point of sale (EFTPOS) terminals.

Stock control

It is important for shops to know how much stock to hold. Too much stock will take up valuable space, is costly and the shop runs the risk of not selling products before their expiry date. Too little stock and customers will be unhappy when they cannot buy what they need! In the store, a database records the stock level for each product. As an item is scanned at the checkout, the number in stock is reduced by one. The store manager decides on how low the stock should get before they reorder more, and they also decide how many to reorder. This information is held in a database.

Internet shopping

Customers can shop from home using the Internet to connect to the supermarket's shopping site. As they connect, the latest products, offers, promotions and prices are downloaded to the customer's computer. After choosing a suitable delivery time, customers browse through the different categories of goods available and place items in the virtual 'trolley'. These are then delivered by the store.

Goods that have been purchased before, either from a previous visit to the store or from earlier Internet orders, are often highlighted to help customers to find the goods they usually buy.

The supermarket Tesco was one of the first to introduce Internet shopping with home delivery from its stores. In the four weeks leading up to Christmas 2006, Tesco delivered 1.3 million orders, which included electronic goods, furniture and many other items as well as groceries. Other companies such as Sainsbury's and Ocado have also set up similar online services.

Loyalty cards

Loyalty cards are issued by supermarkets and promote customer loyalty by awarding points for rewards or discounts. When the card is presented at the checkout, the customer's details, given by the card, are linked with details of the goods purchased. Supermarkets are investing millions of pounds in large mainframe computers with terabytes of data storage. Software is used to build a profile of the customer's buying habits thus allowing the supermarket to target customers with the aim of selling more goods. Sifting through large amounts of data in this way is known as **data mining**.

Bar codes

All goods found on the shelves in supermarkets are labelled with bar codes. The bar codes are formed from a series of black and white lines of varying thickness and represent a 13-digit number, which is also printed under the lines. The number uniquely identifies the type of product and the 13 digits are divided into four groups of numbers showing the country of manufacture, the maker, the product number and a check digit. Bar codes are cheap to produce (just part of the printing on the packaging) and can be read upside-down and on curved surfaces.

The final number of the bar code is a **check digit**, which is calculated mathematically from the other 12 numbers. When the 13 numbers are read, the computer recalculates the check digit and if it is different to the character read by the scanner, the reader will not give the beep to indicate a successful scan. In this situation, the cashier at the till can enter the number manually. A check digit is a validation check ③③▶.

50	10052	01003	7
Represents the country of origin	Manufacturer's number	Product code	Check digit, or check sum, calculated from the other numbers

The use of ICT is essential in a modern police force. Every day, police officers require information about stolen goods, criminals and details of vehicles. They may need to check fingerprints found on a stolen car or check a DNA sample from a murder. This data is all held on computers.

There are 43 police forces in England and Wales, each with their own computer systems. These individual forces are able to share data with other forces across wide area networks. A central computer centre – the Police National Computer (PNC) – also makes valuable data available.

Police communications

With the advances in the technology of mobile telephones, police officers are being equipped with new radios. With these radios, officers can directly access criminal and vehicle databases held on computer and both the voice and the data signals are securely encrypted making them safe from eavesdroppers. The officer's location on patrol can be monitored at the police station and an emergency button on the radio can be used to summon help. The radio network also provides wide national coverage allowing officers to communicate with other forces across the country with a strong, clear signal.

Automatic number plate recognition

If the police wish to check the details of either a vehicle or its owner then they can look this up in the database of vehicles on the computer. Each record in the database uses the vehicle's registration number as a unique key field ⑫. Now, with the advances in digital image decoding software, vehicle registration plates can be recognised by the computer as they pass a camera. These cameras are mounted by the roadside and in the back of police patrol vehicles. Full details for every vehicle are returned from the computer in seconds and, if matches are made with stolen or suspect vehicles, details of the vehicle's location are passed directly to police patrol vehicles. More than 100 000 vehicle checks can be processed each day using this system.

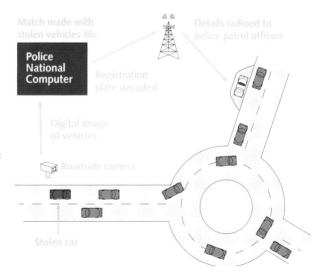

Match made with stolen vehicles file

Details radioed to police patrol officers

Police National Computer

Registration plate decoded

Digital image of vehicles

Roadside camera

Stolen car

Police National Computer

Based at Hendon in London, the PNC came online in 1974 to hold data about criminals and to link with the Drivers Vehicle Licensing Agency (DVLA) computer to provide vehicle information for individual police forces. Today, modern mainframe computers with enormous processing power and data storage link to police stations and mobile terminals in police vehicles across the country. The PNC holds databases on:

- **Criminals** – For everyday police work it is vital for police officers to be able to access information on known criminals. The information held includes:
  - a personal description
  - details of the offence committed
  - details of the arrest
  - known aliases
  - last known address
  - methods used to carry out the offence
  - previous convictions and prison sentences
  - known accomplices.

  This database is called PHOENIX, which stands for Police and Home Office Extended Names IndeX. Descriptive searches can be used to match to criminals in seconds.

- **Vehicle database** – This is the largest database held on the PNC with around 50 million records of vehicles and their owners. The Vehicle Licensing Authority constantly updates the data and, with the latest software, officers around the country can obtain matches within seconds using the partial vehicle descriptions given by witnesses.

- **Fingerprint database** – Fingerprints found at the scene of the crime are photographed and scanned into a computer terminal. The National Automated Fingerprint Identification System (NAFIS) software can compare the prints with those held in the database at the rate of a million per second. The software returns the best matches and a fingerprint specialist then makes the final match. The database currently holds nearly six million sets of ten prints and links directly to the criminal database.

- **DNA database** – The DNA molecule is the biological blueprint for life and the structure of each person's DNA is unique. In the same way that fingerprints found at the scene of a crime can lead to a conviction, so too can minute samples of DNA when analysed and decoded by the forensic team. Over 3.4 million DNA records are held in the database.

- **Stolen property database** – Scotland Yard in London is leading the development of this database with European funding. The database can be accessed worldwide and its aim is to help police trace high-value stolen property. A police officer investigating a theft will enter a description of the stolen property. The software then connects with the different databases in each country and returns small digital images of property that appears to match the description. Selecting these images then produces a full-size picture and a description of the object.

The NPIA (National Policing Improvement Agency) coordinates the development of ICT in the police force (see http://npia.police.uk/).

Major crime investigations

For major crimes, such as murder, large amounts of data are collected by the police. Software is used to coordinate the information and searches are made for similarities with other cases. The latest software, called HOLMES2 (Home Office Large Major Enquiry System 2), enables all the data on the PNC to be accessed and it is able to suggest new lines of inquiry based on the data fed into the system.

The health service uses ICT in many different ways – for the diagnosis of illnesses, in treatment and in the care of patients. It is also used in the administration of hospitals, medical training, in maintaining patients records and in communications between hospitals and surgeries, doctors and nurses.

Diagnosis

Many of the instruments used in hospitals to diagnose illnesses in patients contain embedded computer systems or are linked to computers. The data from sensors attached to patients or from body scans is processed and displayed, enabling doctors to identify problems.

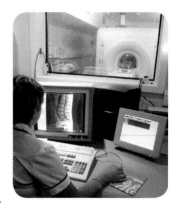

To look for tumours or cancer in a patient, a CAT (computerised axial tomography) scan can be done. A narrow beam of X-rays is passed through the body in thin slices from different directions. A computer builds up a three-dimensional picture of the internal organs without causing any discomfort to the patient.

Monitoring

When people are very ill or have been involved in serious accidents, they are placed in hospital intensive care wards. By using sensors, the patient's condition can be monitored continually, 24 hours a day. These sensors monitor blood pressure, pulse rates, heart waveform, breathing and brain signals. If the incoming data falls above or below set limits, alarms are triggered to alert the doctor and nurses.

Hospital administration

A large hospital may have hundreds of new patients every day. From the moment a patient is admitted into the hospital, computers are used to:

- record their visit
- print labels for medical charts, wrist bands and sample containers
- allocate beds
- timetable expensive resources
- order food
- make appointments and send letters
- prepare staff duty rotas.

Medical training

Computers are used to assist in the training of doctors and nurses. They are used to describe and show the different symptoms of diseases so that doctors can practise diagnosing the illnesses. Simulation software of the human body can show the function of nerves, the circulatory system and the immune system. The computer can simulate the effect of drugs on the body to show how long they are active in the bloodstream. It can show the effect of different doses and the need for repeated doses at specific intervals.

It is vital that doctors have knowledge of the latest medical information and techniques. The Government has introduced a National Library for Health (NLH) to provide easy access to the best current knowledge and know-how. One of the aims of the library is to become one of the 'greatest medical libraries in the world' to help all health care professionals.

Medical records

When a person visits their doctor or goes to hospital, details of their injury or illness and the treatment they receive are recorded in the medical records. A large hospital may hold records for millions of patients. Traditionally, these records were written and stored on paper and held in patient files. Because of the many advantages of holding them electronically, a substantial effort has been made to transfer them into computer databases.

Disadvantages of paper records include:

- They become very bulky, which makes it difficult and time-consuming to find information.
- They are time-consuming for doctors and nurses to complete.
- Storage of bulky folders can cause problems.
- Additional staff need to be employed to retrieve and file records and post them on to other hospitals when patients move.
- With so many folders to look after, there have also been cases of records being lost.

Advantages of computerised records include:

- The record can be searched and data retrieved in a fraction of a second.
- Data can be entered quickly using structured forms onscreen.
- Records occupy very little space.
- Records can be accessed directly from network workstations, in the hospital and from doctors surgeries.
- Records are backed-up for security.
- Different levels of access can be given to administration staff so that they cannot view sensitive data.

An additional advantage of computerised records is the cross-checking of drugs. Certain combinations of drugs can cause problems for patients. When a doctor prescribes a new treatment for a patient, the computer can check that the new medication may be taken safely with any other drugs the patient is already using.

N3

N3 is a project to connect all the doctors surgeries around the country to a computer network linked with hospitals. Eventually, surgeries will be able to book hospital appointments for their patients, receive the results of laboratory tests and access computerised hospital medical records directly from their workstations.

NHS Direct

Lots of medical information is now available to the general public over the Internet. The NHS Direct Web site at www.nhsdirect.nhs.uk provides online information on health features, health care, medical conditions and their treatments. As people are becoming more interested in their own health, the site is very popular and millions of visits are recorded annually.

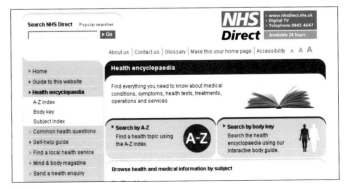

The motor car was invented and put into production many years before computers were available. In the early years of mass production, car manufacturers employed thousands of workers in their factories. Vehicles took many weeks to build and were expensive because of all the wages that had to be paid to the workers. In modern car plants, hundreds of machines – controlled by computers – manufacture, assemble, paint and test the cars.

Design

The manufacturing process starts with the design of the car. Computer aided design software can display 3-D (three-dimensional) images of the car. By simulating the air flow over the car body, the aerodynamics can be tested even before the car is made. The software produces accurate scale drawings for the components that make up the vehicle. The details from these plans can be passed electronically to machines that make the parts. This is known as CAD/CAM ⟨17⟩.

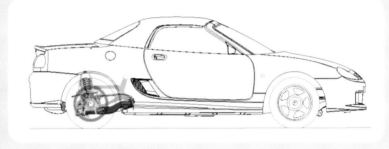

Car manufacture and sales

The traditional approach to manufacturing cars is to use mass production techniques. The aim is to produce as many cars as possible from the factory production lines in the shortest time and car workers on the shop floor are rewarded for increases in productivity (increasing the number of vehicles made). The cars rolling out of the factory are parked, row after row, in huge compounds waiting to be shipped to dealers and sold. This method has disadvantages including:

- Large amounts of money are tied up in the thousands of cars waiting to be sold.
- Customers are becoming increasingly particular about the options they require so it is possible, even with the thousands of cars waiting to be sold, that the 'right' car is not available.

A new and different approach involves the customer making their final decisions about the colour, engine type and optional extras at a workstation. The order is then transmitted to the factory where the car is assembled to the exact specification. The complete process, from order to the delivery of the new car can be achieved in five days and with a reduction in costs of 30%.

Car assembly

The building of a car starts with welding the body panels together. This car shell is then given a protective coating to stop rust before the upholstery, seats, dashboard, engine and suspension units are fitted. The car is then painted and fitted with windows and wheels ready for testing.

Throughout the assembly process, computerised robots are used for lifting and moving parts, welding the body panels and paint spraying. Large factories use over a thousand robots to perform these tasks.

Robots

The first robot to be used in manufacturing was in 1962 at the General Motors factory in the US. Now there are an estimated 800 000 robots worldwide.

Robot arms (23)▶ can be powered by:

- **Hydraulic rams** – Rams and pistons operated by oil, very powerful, good for lifting.
- **Pneumatic rams** – Rams and pistons operated by compressed air, good for welding and paint spraying, very fast.
- **Electric motors** – Good for intricate work, accurate and precise.

The initial purchase and installation of automated machinery is expensive, but robots have many advantages including:

- low running costs
- continuous operation, 24 hours per day, without tiring or the need for breaks
- faster operations: a robotic arm can average one weld per second
- consistent and accurate work (eg welding body panels)
- the ability to handle heavy loads (eg lifting car engines)
- the ability to work in hostile environments (eg paint spraying areas).

Since the first robots were built, they have evolved to become aware of their surroundings. This evolution has been classified into generations:

- **First generation** – These had no input sensors so, for a welding robot, if the car was not in the correct position the weld was made in mid-air!
- **Second generation** – These included sensors that made them 'aware' of their surroundings.
- **Third generation** – The latest robots under development use artificial intelligence software to adapt and reason with the incoming data in order to improve their performance.

Working from home

You may have learnt in history about the Industrial Revolution where people flocked from the countryside to find work in the towns and cities. Now, the information technology revolution is reversing that trend by allowing people to move away from towns and cities and work from homes in the country. The number of people working from home instead of a company office has been rising steadily. In 2005, over 3 million people, 11% of the UK workforce worked from home. What makes home working possible are the advances in ICT. The cost of the equipment necessary to work effectively from home is affordable for many employers and the advantages to both the worker and the company can be considerable.

The photo above illustrates some of the equipment that might be used for home working. Being able to communicate with the office, work colleagues and, in some cases, with customers is vitally important. A fast way of accessing the Internet for receiving emails and video conferencing can be achieved through a broadband connection.

Security

When companies have Internet connections into the internal network, it is very important to protect against unauthorised access by hackers. Some companies issue **biometric devices**, like thumbprint scanners, to home workers to use instead of relying on passwords when logging on. Home workers browsing the Internet are also more likely to pick up viruses because they probably have less protection on their computers than office systems do. Employers need to ensure their home workers have the latest anti-virus software installed on their machines.

Why work from home?

Working from home has improved the quality of life for many people. They no longer have to spend hours travelling to work, sitting in traffic jams or relying on public transport. They can avoid the noise and bustle of the city office and, instead, enjoy the comforts of home. Usually, working hours can be more flexible to fit in with other commitments, for example, taking children to and from school.

There are also good reasons for the employer to encourage home working. When new staff need to be recruited, it may not always be possible to find staff with the right skills living locally or willing to travel to the office. Home working makes it easier to recruit staff with the right skills from anywhere in the country and removes the need to pay high salaries and relocation expenses. The increase in the quality of life offered by home working is important to workers and they may accept lower salaries in exchange. Companies also save money by having smaller offices; the saving in city office space can be as much as £6000 per worker per year.

Employers need to provide the right facilities to make home working effective. One problem for workers is the feeling of isolation when they operate from home. Employers can use video conferencing over the Internet so that workers can interact more effectively. Web pages with company information and news can also be created for workers to access from home. These Web pages, which are held on the company's computer and are only used within the organisation, are called an **intranet**.

Some of the advantages and disadvantages of home working for the worker are:

Advantages to the home worker

+ Improved quality of life.

+ No stress of travelling to the office.

+ Travelling time saved.

+ Cost of travelling saved.

+ Greater flexibility of working hours.

+ Increased self-esteem by being trusted to work at home.

+ Can be at home with children.

Disadvantages to the home worker

− Possible feeling of isolation.

− No social contact with fellow workers.

Some of the advantages and disadvantages of home working for the employer are:

Advantages to the employer

+ Saves cost of office space.

+ Greater loyalty from employees because of the trust given to them.

+ Often workers increase the amount of work they do from home – increased productivity.

Disadvantages to the employer

− More difficult to build teams and share and generate ideas between colleagues.

− Additional cost of home working equipment and Internet connection charges.

− Greater need for security against hacking and viruses.

Growth of computing

If you have a chance to visit the computing section at the Science Museum, you will see how very recent the development of computers is. Engines, cars and motorcycles were invented over a hundred years ago and, in comparison with the development of computers, they have changed very little.

We take computers for granted. However, our grandparents were brought up in a society where computers were only used in large businesses and were very expensive. These early electronic computers, using glass tubes called valves, were constructed around 60 years ago. These first computers were used to calculate firing tables for field guns and to crack German codes during the war. Their processing power was very small by today's standards and the machines filled large rooms and consumed enormous quantities of power. The widespread use of computers in homes, schools and businesses only began about 30 years ago. Today, this growth continues; month by month, computers become more sophisticated, have larger memories, better displays, faster processing, new features; yet, prices remain the same or even decrease.

Effect of ICT on society

Computers have an enormous impact on our lives. Some people long for the 'good old days' before computers, when the pace of life was slower and less complicated. Others are greatly attracted by the opportunities this new technology offers. Life as we know it today, however, could not exist if this modern technology were removed. Without the aid

of computerised technology, it would not be possible to handle all the bank cheques written every day or the millions of telephone calls made. Our standard of living would fall, prices would rise and any country that adopted this approach would fail in the competitive world in which we live.

The Internet, email and the use of mobile phones have changed the way in which we communicate. The use of technology is beginning to reverse the trend started during the Industrial Revolution when people moved from the countryside into the towns to find work. With modern communications systems, people are now moving back into the country and are able to work from home.

It was once said that the use of computers would lead to the paperless office. However, computers are responsible for generating more printed material than ever before. The computerised mail delivered to our homes (eg bills, forms, advertising leaflets, junk mail) shows that there is a lot of information about people held on computer files. Some of this data is confidential (for example, medical and financial records) and not all of it is accurate.

ICT is changing the nature of employment. When your grandparents were young, people often kept the same job throughout their working life. These days, many people change professions several times during their career and the need to be flexible and undertake retraining is important. The introduction of computers has led to the loss of many jobs, particularly in manufacturing, but it has also created new jobs and the need for new skills.

Jobs lost

Where jobs can be done by computers or computerised machines, many workers have lost their jobs. Machines have low running costs in comparison with workers' wages so goods cost less to make. Machines are also able to run continuously, without breaks or sleep, and they work quickly and accurately.

Jobs have also been lost in offices. Before the widespread use of computers, people were employed as filing clerks to manage the office documents. Now, documents generated on the word processor are stored directly on hard disk drives of computers. In banks, thousands of staff were employed at the counters to issue cash to customers. Their jobs have now been replaced by the computerised cash machines (ATMs) (4).

Jobs gained

There have been many jobs created within the computer industry. New factories have been built to manufacture computers and computer peripherals like printers. New shops, retail outlets and dealerships have been created and software and training companies have been established.

Within existing companies, workers have needed to retrain and improve their computing skills to handle new systems and processes. In the past, junior office staff may only have needed to learn to type. In today's office, staff need skills in word processing, databases and spreadsheets. They may need to be able to email documents, purchase online, edit Web pages, mailmerge letters and understand how to store data safely.

Computers have been responsible for increased productivity at work and for many people this has resulted in a higher standard of living. People have more money and time for sport and leisure activities and for taking holidays. This has led to new jobs in the service industry; in catering, hotels, sport and travel.

Social interaction

With the development of the Internet and the advances in ICT, the patterns of people's lives are changing. There is an increase in people working from home and communicating with the office by telephone, the Internet and email. There is no need to go out to shop; online shopping will deliver your supermarket shop to the door and clothes and household goods can all be purchased over the Internet. Goods can be paid for by credit card, bank accounts can be viewed and payments made by home banking over the Internet. These developments are reducing the need for social interaction with others.

Environment

Computers generate a lot of paper and many trees have been cut down and power used to make paper that is often wasted. Some businesses have made a real effort to create the 'paperless' office but companies that generate 'junk' mail are wasting precious resources. Using ICT to control heating systems and manufacturing processes can often save resources. ICT also allows people to work from home which cuts fuel use and car pollution.

Communications

It was only a few years ago that students studied IT at school, not ICT. The introduction of the word 'communication' reflects the huge changes that have occurred in society through recent developments in technology. Now, the majority of people in the UK have mobile phones and can be contacted instantly. Sending text messages, and the 'text messaging language' that has evolved from using the number pad on the phone, was unheard of ten years ago. For young people, the Internet offers instant communication with messaging software, like MSN, and chat rooms. Email messages and attachments have become a vital form of communication in business; a generation ago, almost all written communications were sent by post taking days for documents to pass between companies.

Business

Nearly all businesses use ICT to some extent. For many businesses, a computer failure for any length of time would be very damaging, if not fatal, to their operation. The Internet has become an important means of advertising and selling products and many companies have their Web site address prominently displayed on their company vehicles. The Internet provides the same opportunity to the one man sole trader as it does to a large corporation – the cost of hosting a Web site is the same and the potential customers you can reach are the whole world's Internet population! To reach this audience, some Web sites offer a choice of languages on their home page, for example, one Internet bookshop offers users a choice of 13 languages.

ICT in society – 2

Education

Computers are a valuable tool in education and the ratio of students to computers in secondary schools has fallen from 10:1 in 1994 to 4:1 in 2005. Pupils and teachers use computers across the curriculum. Computers are used with interactive whiteboards (shown on the right), digital projectors and to access the resources of the Internet. The MFL department can use video conferencing facilities to link with pupils in schools abroad, the science department can use remote data logging and the design and technology department can operate CAD/CAM lathes.

Health

highlighted some of the benefits of ICT in the health service with the monitoring of patients, diagnosis of illness, training of doctors, storage of medical records and the administration of hospitals. Computerised machines perform tasks that are potentially dangerous for people. For example, paint spraying cars, lifting heavy loads, deep sea exploration or working in contaminated or radioactive areas. Although computers can be beneficial to our health, we must also remember that working with computers can cause eye strain, headaches, back problems and RSI (repetitive strain injury) 53 .

Crime

To help fight crime, the development of ICT systems has improved the tools available to police forces around the country 46 . Companies that used to pay workers their wages in cash now transfer the money electronically to their bank accounts and, as people use credit cards to pay for goods, there is a lot less cash about to be stolen. Plastic card fraud, however, is still a problem. There are well over 100 million plastic cards being used in the UK and each year hundreds of millions of pounds are stolen by criminals through lost or stolen cards and, to a smaller extent, by copying (counterfeiting) cards. However, the use of integrated chip cards has helped reduce the problem.

Privacy

Many people are concerned about the personal information held on computers. With wide area networks like the Internet, data can be transmitted around the world in minutes. Many organisations hold data about individuals. For example, Government census data, income tax office, pension companies, banks, building societies, supermarkets through loyalty cards, credit card companies, the DVLA (Driver and Vehicle Licensing Agency) and insurance companies. Quite detailed profiles of individuals can be collected from this data and, if data is entered inaccurately, people may find, for example, they are refused credit when making purchases. The Data Protection Act 52 was designed to protect the rights of individuals.

The Data Protection Act, 1998

The 'right to privacy' is a right we all expect. We do not expect personal details such as our age, medical records, personal family details, political and religious beliefs to be freely available to everybody. With the growth of information and communication technology, large databases are able to hold huge quantities of information and global networks are able to share and distribute this information around the world in seconds. To protect people and their personal information, the Data Protection Act was formed. The first Act was made law in 1984 but was replaced by a new Act in 1998 to include the European Union law.

If any person, organisation, company or business wishes to hold personal information about people, they must register with the Office of the Information Commissioner.

The Data Protection Act contains eight basic principles. A summary of these is shown below:

Personal data

Personal data is data that can identify a living person and allow an opinion to be expressed about that person. For example, just a name and address is not considered personal data. If the data also includes their date of birth and earnings this is considered personal data.

The data can be further classified as 'sensitive' personal data if it includes details of a person's:

- racial or ethnic origins
- religious beliefs
- their physical or mental health or condition
- political opinions
- trade union membership
- sexual life.

Note: One big change between the 1984 version of the Act and the 1998 version is that manual records (not kept on a computer) are now subject to legislation.

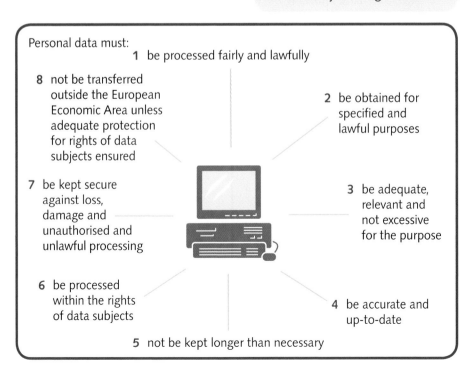

Personal data must:

1 be processed fairly and lawfully

8 not be transferred outside the European Economic Area unless adequate protection for rights of data subjects ensured

2 be obtained for specified and lawful purposes

7 be kept secure against loss, damage and unauthorised and unlawful processing

3 be adequate, relevant and not excessive for the purpose

6 be processed within the rights of data subjects

4 be accurate and up-to-date

5 not be kept longer than necessary

Rights of data subjects

In the sixth of the eight principles shown, the rights of the data subject were mentioned. The rights of individuals increased substantially in the 1998 Act. The individual can:

- be given a copy of the data held
- prevent processing of the data if it is likely to cause damage or distress
- prevent the data being used for direct marketing
- prevent automated decisions being made on the basis of data held
- receive compensation for damage and distress caused by use of the data
- have data corrected, blocked and erased if inaccurate
- make a request to the Information Commissioner if they feel the Act has been contravened.

The Computer Misuse Act, 1990

Hacking, computer fraud and computer viruses ⟨35⟩ are all relatively new crimes that established English laws were not designed to deal with. For example, under existing laws, a hacker could only be prosecuted for the theft of electricity. To deal with these new crimes, a law was introduced in 1990 called The Computer Misuse Act. Under this law, the following offences could be dealt with:

- **Hacking** – Unauthorised access to any program or data held in a computer. Penalty is a maximum fine of £5000 and a six-month prison sentence.
- **Computer fraud and blackmail** – Penalty is an unlimited fine and a maximum five-year prison sentence.
- **Viruses** – Unauthorised modification of the contents of a computer, impairing the operation of any program or reliability of data. Penalty is an unlimited fine and a maximum five-year prison sentence.

Exemptions

There are exemptions to the Act and exemptions in the rules governing the need to register data. These include data that is:

- related to national security
- associated with crime and taxation
- involved in health, education and social work
- used in regulatory activities by public 'watch dogs'
- processed for special (journalistic, literary and artistic) purposes
- used in research, history and statistics
- required by law and in connection with legal proceedings being disclosed
- held for domestic purposes, eg household, personal and family affairs.

The Copyright, Designs and Patents Act, 1988

Copying computer software, or software piracy, is now a criminal offence under this 1988 Act. The Act covers stealing software, using illegally-copied software and manuals, and running purchased software on two or more machines at the same time without a suitable licence. Organisations purchase software licences to cover the number of workstations on their network but sometimes they neglect to purchase additional licences as they buy more workstations.

The legal penalties for breaking the copyright law include unlimited fines and up to two years in prison.

It has been estimated that half the software used is copied illegally. In the UK, two organisations have been formed to stop the illegal use of software:

- **FAST (Federation Against Software Theft),** founded in 1984, is a non-profit organisation to promote the legal use of software.
- **BSA (Business Software Alliance)** exists to make organisations and their employees aware of the law and encourage its implementation.

It is important to realise that working with computers, particularly for long periods of time, can be dangerous to your health. To create a safe working environment, the following factors should be considered.

Room and furniture design

The safest environment is a tidy and well-organised room. Electrical cables should not trail across the floor, and food and drinks should be kept well away from the computer and keyboard. Computers should be positioned so that sunlight from the window does not reflect on the screen. Sitting at a computer for long periods of time is never comfortable. Leaning back in the chair reduces the pressure on the spine but then the arms have to reach forward to the keyboard creating muscle tension which leads to aches and pains in the neck, shoulders, back and arms. Sitting upright with the feet flat, the upper arms straight down, parallel with the body, and the lower arms horizontal resting on the keyboard is the best posture. Adjustable chairs that give maximum support for the back are best. The illustration on the right shows correct and incorrect positions for working at a computer.

Even with a comfortable working environment, it is still good to stand up, stretch, move and look out of the window to relieve the eyes every 15 minutes when working at a computer.

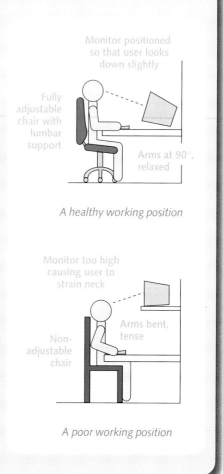

Monitor positioned so that user looks down slightly

Fully adjustable chair with lumbar support

Arms at 90°, relaxed

A healthy working position

Monitor too high causing user to strain neck

Arms bent, tense

Non-adjustable chair

A poor working position

Monitor

Staring at a computer monitor for long periods can lead to eye strain and headaches. Large monitors with high resolutions are easier on the eyes. All new monitors must comply with EU standards which ensure that radiation emission is as low as possible.

The Health and Safety (Display Screen Equipment) Regulations 1992: These regulations were introduced by the Government to protect workers who use computer monitors in their work. The legislation requires employers to ensure that the workstation and the environment is safe and workers take frequent breaks or change activity often. If employees spend a significant amount of time at their workstation, the employer must pay for workers to have eye tests.

Keyboard

The standard keyboard, known as the QWERTY keyboard because of the arrangement of letters along the top row, is not a logical layout. The keyboard design is over 100 years old and was designed to reduce the typing speed so that the letters on the original mechanical typewriters did not jam. The layout is now so well established that it is difficult to change but it has led to serious health problems for some typists. These workers suffer from neck, arm and hand pains called RSI (repetitive strain injury) or, as it is becoming more commonly known, WRULD (work-related upper limb disorder). Ergonomically-designed keyboards, where the keys are split and contoured for the hands, can be purchased with prices ranging from £20 to over £100.

Wrist support

Supporting the wrist

Right   Wrong

Electrical considerations

Computers are generally connected to 240V mains electricity and must be treated with care. The computer should be properly earthed and the plugs should be fitted with the correct fuses. If the computer is moved or opened, the power cable should be the first to be disconnected and the last to be reconnected. In case of a fire, the fire extinguishers should be powder-based or CO_2 (carbon dioxide) devices. Water-based fire extinguishers should **not** be used on electrical appliances.

Safety and the Internet

Another aspect of safety when using computers concerns use of the Internet. The Internet is completely unregulated, there are Web sites with information from aardvarks (Afrikaans for 'earth pig') to zymurgy (the art of fermentation). Together with the many interesting and educational pages, there are also sites containing undesirable material like illegal pornography. Even quite ordinary and innocent searches for information can unearth these sites and young children need to be protected from viewing them.

In schools, Internet service providers, like Research Machines, provide a comprehensive filtering service to stop pupils viewing inappropriate material. These services cannot guarantee 100% blocking as the Internet is a continually changing environment but as new undesirable sites are found they are blocked.

At home, although filtering software can be purchased, it is still advisable that access to the Internet is made under the supervision of parents.

Before taking your ICT examination, you should practise with questions from books and past papers. This section gives you some general advice and hints on answering questions.

Do's and don'ts

Do:	Don't:
• make sure you have answered all the questions, check every page including the back page • read the questions carefully and give an answer to what is being asked, not something else.	• repeat the question as part of your answer • leave out any questions • write more than the space or lines provided for the answer • waffle.

A question may ask for a specific number of points or reasons; you should only give the number of answers asked for. If you do not know the answer to a question then make a sensible guess, you cannot lose marks for incorrect answers. If the question asks you to ring two items in a list and you do not know the answer, ring the two that seem most likely – do not ring more than the question asks. If you are asked for an advantage and a disadvantage, do not make one the opposite of the other – choose different points.

Words used in questions

Different key words are used in examination questions and they each require different types of answer. Key words include:

Answers becoming longer and more detailed

These are usually short statements that answer the question. This is the only occasion where a one-word answer may obtain a mark, for example:

Example question 1

Part of an art database is shown below:

Exhibit number	Type	Title	Artist	Value
1089	Watercolour	Lucy's Visit	Coglan	£150
1090	Oil	A Karlstad Student	Gille	£175
1091	Print	Gates of Woodbridge	Shelley	£210
1092	Print	Lison's Sunset	Gille	£150

a **State** how many records are shown.

............4............... (1)

b For each record, **state** how many fields are shown.

............5............... (1)

give

You must provide a little more information in your answers than a single word.

Example question 2

Give two benefits to an employee of working from home:

Benefit 1 *The working hours are often more flexible.* (1)

Benefit 2 *Time and money are saved by not travelling to the office.* (1)

describe

You must be able to describe the answer to the question in clear sentences. The length of the description will depend on the space provided for the answer and the number of marks given for the question.

Example question 3

In the art database table (see question 1) the 'Exhibit number' is the *key field*. **Describe** what is meant by a *key field*.

The key field is used to identify the record. It contains a unique entry and is often used when searching and sorting records. (2)

Timing

This is important; if your answers are rushed and you find yourself finishing the paper half an hour early then you may have lost important marks where detail is missing and from the marks awarded for spelling, punctuation and grammar. The following example shows how some understanding of timing can help.

A recent Edexcel GCSE ICT paper was divided into three sections as follows: Section A = 20 marks, Section B = 43 marks, Section C = 63 marks: Total = 126 marks.

2 hours (ie 120 minutes) was allowed for the exam. Allowing for ten minutes to read the paper, this works out at just under a minute a mark. A question worth five marks should take a little under five minutes to answer.

explain

This is similar to 'describe' but you should also think about the advantages and the disadvantages of the situation and include these if appropriate. Make sure that for each point you write about it is clear whether this is an advantage or a disadvantage. Sometimes you will only be asked to explain one side, eg 'explain the benefits of' or 'explain the problems with'. When you are asked to explain something, don't answer with phrases like 'it's quicker' or 'it's easier' or 'it's cheaper', etc without explaining **why**.

Example question 4

When entering data into a database it can be validated. **Explain** what is meant by data validation.

This is a check on the data made by the software when the data is input. A number of different checks can be made. All are designed to see if the data entered is sensible. (3)

discuss

When you are asked to discuss a situation, start with an explanation, including (if appropriate) the advantages and disadvantages. You may be asked to finish with a conclusion giving your view, either for or against, but make sure you have a reasoned argument.

Example question 5

Discuss the advantages and disadvantages of using information technology in shopping.

The use of bar codes on products is an advantage because the products can be read quickly by the laser scanner at the checkout tills and this reduces the queuing time for customers. Computerised systems produce itemised till receipts for the customer and manage stock control for the shop manager. A disadvantage of using IT is the reliance placed on the systems. If the system 'crashes' then it can be chaotic in large stores. Staff have also been made redundant. (6)

Use the answer grid at the end of the questions to record your answers. Check your answers by using the completed grid at the back of the book.

Hardware

1 Forecasting the weather requires enormous computing power. What type of computer is used?
   a Embedded computer
   b Mainframe computer
   c PDA
   d Supercomputer

2 What kind of input devices are used with embedded computers to control systems?
   a Sensors
   b Bar code readers
   c MICR
   d Keyboards

3 A student deleted his document file on the computer by mistake. He had no back-up of the file but he did have a printed copy. What input device could be used to recreate the work in a word processor?
   a Touch screen
   b Scanner with OCR software
   c Braille keyboard
   d Graphic tablet and stylus

4 Which of the following input devices is not used by banks?
   a MIDI
   b MICR
   c Smart cards
   d Magnetic stripes

5 Which of the following are both output devices?
   a Digital camera and plotter
   b Bar code reader and monitor
   c Plotter and flat panel monitor
   d Printer and microphone

6 P, Q and R describe three printers.
   P – A quiet, high quality, black and white printer suitable for desktop publishing work.
   Q – A colour printer for use at home.
   R – An impact printer that can print several copies at once using self-carbonating paper.
   Match the printer to the correct description.
   a Dot-matrix printer – P
   b Ink-jet – R
   c Dot-matrix printer – Q
   d Laser – P

7 In a factory warehouse, what type of printer is needed to print multiple copies using sheets of self-carbonating paper?
   a Ink-jet   b Bubble-jet
   c Laser   d Dot-matrix

8 If you bought an encyclopedia in computerised form, it would most likely be stored on:
   a a CD-ROM
   b a RAM chip
   c a hard disk
   d magnetic tape

9 A unit of computer memory is called:
   a Byte   b Megahertz
   c RAM   d Check digit

10 The illustration shows the basic operation of a computer.

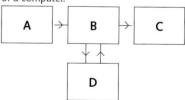

Which letter is correctly labelled?
   a D – Input
   b B – Process
   c C – Backing store
   d A – Output

11 A doctor's receptionist is asked to store information about each patient on a computer. The software application most suitable for this is:

a a computer aided design package

b a spreadsheet package

c a desktop publishing package

d a database package

12 A database is used to store the details of cars in the car park. One record is shown below.

Make	Ford
Model	Fiesta
Registration number	P727WTN
Colour	Red
Owner (Surname)	Wallace
Owner (Initial)	R
Room	L2-34

Which field would be the best choice for the key field?

a Owner (Surname)

b Registration number

c Room

d Make

13 The most sensible coding for a gender field in a database is:

a F   M

b 1   0

c %   &

d Female   Male

14 A database record structure is:

a the number of records in a file

b the name, length and type of each field in a record

c the length of a record

d the number of files on a disk

15 Using a desktop publishing package, an article is set out using three columns:

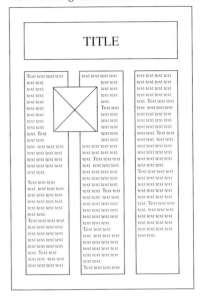

Which of the following options will not expand the text to fill the page?

a Increase the font size

b Increase the picture frame

c Decrease the title frame

d Decrease the column widths

16 Microsoft® Paint creates bitmap images. Which of the following statements is true?

a Bitmap images take up a lot of memory

b The paint program uses vector graphics

c The edges are still smooth when you zoom in

d A bitmap picture is also called a pixel

17 Web pages are created using HTML code. Which of the following statements is not true?

a HTML stands for hypertext markup language

b HTML tags are enclosed by < and >

c HTML files have file extensions .web

d HTML tags are usually found in pairs

18 For the first six months of the year the sales of chocolate bars from the tuck shop are recorded in a spreadsheet. This is shown at the bottom of the page.
A mistake is found for the Bounty sales in May (cell F4) and this is changed from 65 to 55. When the spreadsheet recalculates:
a all the values in row 4 will change
b only the value in F4 will change
c all the values in column F will change
d the values in cells F4, F7 and H4 will change

19 Computer modelling helps people to make decisions. Which Microsoft program is used for computer modelling?
a Internet Explorer
b Microsoft® Excel
c Microsoft® Access
d Outlook Express

20 A robot arm, used to weld car body panels, incorporates sensors to ensure the weld is made in the correct place. The process of monitoring input signals that affect the output data is called:
a embedded
b actuator
c feedback
d pneumatic

21 Control instructions are written to move a machine from point A to point B:

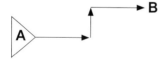

FD – forward
LT – left
RT – right
The left and right commands are followed by the angle of turn in degrees.

Select the correct set of instructions:
a FD 100, LT 90, FD 50, LT 90, FD 100
b FD 100, LT 90, FD 50, RT 90, FD 100
c FD 100, RT 90, FD 50, RT 90, FD 100
d FD 100, FD 50, FD 100, LT 90

22 A computer-controlled greenhouse uses sensors to maintain the ideal growing conditions for the plants. Control systems include:
• heaters to control the temperature
• window blinds to control the light level.
Which two input sensors are required?
a LDR and thermistor
b Thermistor and switch
c Light pen and thermistor
d LDR and actuator

23 Which of the following situations does not use real-time processing?
a An embedded computer-controlled washing machine
b Asking directory enquiries for a telephone number
c A flight simulator package
d Printing salary payslips

24 The Microsoft® Windows operating system provides a graphical user interface (GUI). Which of the following is not part of a GUI environment?
a Icons
b Menus
c WIMP
d Command line

25 In software development one of the stages in the system life cycle is the implementation stage. This is when:
a a written copy of the solution is prepared
b the software is used with data
c a feasibility study is carried out
d you state the improvements that could be made

(see Question 18)
Tuck shop sales

	A	B	C	D	E	F	G	H
1		Jan	Feb	Mar	Apr	May	Jun	Total
2	Mars Bar	144	156	141	135	122	126	824
3	Snickers	86	76	88	93	91	104	538
4	Bounty	66	58	44	53	65	55	341
5	Aero	46	53	38	42	62	56	297
6	KitKat	155	152	142	147	138	147	881
7	Total	497	495	453	470	478	488	

Data

26 ASCII code:

    a was used during the war to send messages

    b is an Internet search engine

    c is a code for keyboard characters

    d is a type of bar code

27 A computer has 32 MB (megabytes) of RAM. How many bytes is this?

    a 32 000 000

    b 32×10^6

    c 33 554 432

    d 32 102 400

28 A database for holding contact details is created using fixed length fields.

Field name	Size
Title	4
Initial	2
Surname	20
Telephone	12
Email address	40

How many bytes of memory would the file use if there were 100 records in the file?

    a 5000

    b 6800

    c 7000

    d 7800

29 What method of data capture has replaced magnetic stripes on bank cards to reduce the possibility of fraud?

    a ICC

    b MICR

    c OCR

    d OMR

30 When you change your password on the network you are asked to confirm the change by typing the new password twice. This is an example of:

    a verification

    b validation

    c data entry

    d synchronisation

31 Some numbers are given an extra digit, called a check digit, as a validation check. Using the UPC method, calculate the check digit for 3427.

    a 2

    b 6

    c 7

    d 9

32–34 A transport company collects data (fuel, mileage details, etc) daily from each of its lorries and enters this into the computer. Each week it updates the vehicle master file and prints reports for the managers. This process is illustrated:

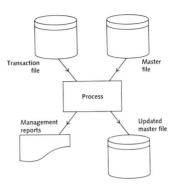

32 The flow chart shown is a:

    a data flow chart

    b system flow chart

    c program flow chart

    d binary flow chart

33 Before the transaction file is merged with the master file during the update process, it must be:

    a formatted

    b sorted

    c compressed

    d printed

34 The updated master file is known as:

    a grandfather

    b father

    c son

    d daughter

35 A network manager gives a file the security permissions RW. This means that users:

    a have no access

    b can delete the file

    c can read and write to the file

    d can read and delete the file

Networks

36 Which of the following statements is true
    about computer networks?
    a There is a greater threat from
       computer viruses
    b Computer peripherals cannot be shared
    c Ring topology networks are the
       most common
    d LAN stands for large area network

37 The diagram below shows five
    workstations connected to a
    network server.

(C = computer)

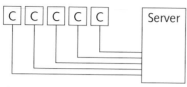

The network topology shown is a:
    a chain
    b ring
    c bus
    d star

38 Direct line of sight is required for data
    transmission with:
    a microwave
    b fibre optic
    c ISDN
    d UTP cable

39 Which of the following ways is most likely
    to be used to connect LAN stations?
    a Satellite
    b Microwave
    c UTP cable
    d Fibre optic

40 When connecting a computer to
    the Internet which of the following
    are required?
    a ISP + Web browser
    b Web browser + CD-ROM drive
    c Modem + Microsoft® Office software
    d ISP + printer

41 A useful tool when researching
    information from the Internet is:
    a search engine
    b virtual trolley
    c CD-ROM
    d user manual

42 Which device is used for the instant
    transmission of a printed document?
    a Post
    b Fax
    c Text message
    d Telephone

43 A Web cam is a necessary piece of
    equipment for:
    a sending a fax
    b sending an email
    c video conferencing
    d sending a document attachment

44 WAP (wireless application protocol) is
    associated with:
    a mobile phones
    b spam emails
    c codec cards
    d network cards

45 Which of the following is not required for
    video conferencing?
    a Web cam
    b Microphone
    c Computer
    d Search engine

Applications of ICT

46 When withdrawing cash from an ATM,
    what do you need as well as a bank card?
    a Cheque book
    b Bank statement
    c PIN
    d Passport

47 Cheques supplied by banks to their
    customers have three sets of MICR
    characters printed along the bottom.
    These characters contain details of:
    a customer name/account number/bank
       sort code
    b cheque number/account number/bank
       sort code
    c bank sort code/date/account number
    d customer name/account number/date

48 When a cheque is cashed at the bank, the
    bank staff:
    a type the details into the computer
    b print a fourth number onto the cheque
    c wait three days before sending the
       cheque to BACS
    d erase the MICR numbers

49 The process of transferring money electronically over a computer network when paying for goods by credit or debit card at a supermarket is called:

  a EFT   b EFP

  c BACS   d FAST

50–51 Details of the goods sold in a supermarket are stored in a database. The illustration at the bottom of the page shows the data stored for several products.

50 Which produce needs to be reordered?

  a Assam tea

  b Spaghetti rings

  c Baked beans

  d Chopped tomatoes

51 With reference to the database below, when the stock of peas is low, how many will be reordered?

  a 96   b 112

  c 312   d 340

52 Which of the following acronyms is not associated with the police force?

  a NPIA   b BACS

  c PHOENIX   d HOLMES

53 The approximate number of records in the PNC vehicle database is:

  a 30 million   b 40 million

  c 50 million   d 60 million

54 In the health service, patients' medical records are being transferred onto computer. Select the correct statement:

  a Information is easier to find in paper records

  b Paper records take up very little space

  c Computer records can only be accessed from a single workstation

  d Computer records use structured forms making them easier for staff to complete

55 Because of ICT, more people are now able to work from home. When people work from home:

  a There is more stress with increased travelling

  b The quality of life is often decreased

  c There is greater flexibility of working hours

  d Their children should be at school

Effects of ICT

56 Under which law is it an offence to create and distribute a computer virus?

  a The Data Protection Act, 1998

  b The Computer Misuse Act, 1990

  c The Copyright, Designs and Patents Act, 1988

  d Display Screen Equipment Regulation, 1992

57 On how many principles is the Data Protection Act based?

  a 8   b 9

  c 11   d 14

58 In the Data Protection Act, which of the following is not considered personal information? A person's:

  a name and address

  b political opinion

  c religious beliefs

  d ethnic origin

59 When using a computer keyboard for long periods of time people can suffer from RSI. This stands for:

  a Resolution of Screen Images

  b Repetitive Strain Injury

  c Rapid Stress Indicator

  d Read and Speech Injury

60 The type of fire extinguisher suitable for use with computer equipment is:

  a water-based   b CO_2

  c oxygen   d none

Supermarket goods (see Questions 50–51)

Product code	Description	Quantity in stock	Minimum stock level	Reorder quantity
235367	Baked beans (tin)	255	240	96
235388	Peas (tin)	340	312	112
236210	Chopped tomatoes (tin)	128	144	48
236268	Assam tea (pkt)	56	40	24
236330	Spaghetti rings (tin)	243	212	96

Answer grid

Question	a	b	c	d
1				
2				
3				
4				
5				
6				
7				
8				
9				
10				
11				
12				
13				
14				
15				
16				
17				
18				
19				
20				
21				
22				
23				
24				
25				
26				
27				
28				
29				
30				

Question	a	b	c	d
31				
32				
33				
34				
35				
36				
37				
38				
39				
40				
41				
42				
43				
44				
45				
46				
47				
48				
49				
50				
51				
52				
53				
54				
55				
56				
57				
58				
59				
60				

Index

Answers

Question	a	b	c	d
1				X
2	X			
3		X		
4	X			
5			X	
6				X
7				X
8	X			
9	X			
10		X		
11				X
12		X		
13	X			
14		X		
15			X	
16	X			
17			X	
18				X
19		X		
20			X	
21		X		
22	X			
23				X
24				X
25		X		
26			X	
27			X	
28				X
29	X			
30	X			

Question	a	b	c	d
31	X			
32		X		
33		X		
34			X	
35			X	
36	X			
37				X
38	X			
39			X	
40	X			
41	X			
42		X		
43		X		
44	X			
45				X
46		X		
47		X		
48		X		
49	X			
50				X
51		X		
52		X		
53			X	
54				X
55			X	
56		X		
57	X			
58	X			
59		X		
60		X		

Topic to syllabus table

The table below is an approximate guide to match the syllabuses from the different examination boards with the topics in the handbook. Syllabuses are presented in a variety of ways; some are very detailed, while others are much more general. Teachers are recommended to carry out a more detailed analysis for the particular syllabus they are using.

Key: • = Included in the syllabus
  ○ = Mentioned in the syllabus but not specific
  Blank cell = Not included in the syllabus

Section	Topic	AQA A	AQA B	Edexcel	OCR A	WJEC	CCEA
1	Types of computer	•	•	•	•	•	•
	Supercomputer					•	
	Mainframe computer		•		•	•	
	Microcomputer	•	•	•	•	•	•
	Notebooks		•		•	•	
	Personal digital assistants		•		•	•	
	Embedded computers		•		•	•	
2	Input devices: Physical	•	•	•	•	•	•
	Keyboard	•	•	•	○	•	•
	Braille keyboard	•			○	•	
	Concept keyboard	•		•	○	•	
	Mouse	•	•	•	•	•	•
	Trackerball	•	•	•	•		•
	Joystick	•	•		•	•	•
	Graphics tablet	•		•	•	•	
	Touch pad	•	•		•	•	
3	Input devices: Light	•	•	•	•	•	•
	Optical mark reader (OMR)	•	•	•	•	•	•
	Scanner	•	•	•	•	•	•
	Optical character recognition (OCR)	•	•	•	•	•	•
	Bar code reader	•	•	•	•	•	
	Touch screen	•	•	•	•	•	•
	Light pen	•				•	
	Digital camera and Web cam	•	•	•	•	•	•
	Video capture	•			•	•	
4	Other input devices	•	•	•	•	•	•
	Magnetic ink character recognition (MICR)	•	•		•	•	
	Magnetic stripe	•	•	•	•	•	•
	Smart card					•	•
	Microphone	•	•	•	•	•	•
	Musical instrument digital interface (MIDI)				•	•	
	Sensors (switches, thermistors, LDRs)	•	•	•	•	•	•
5	Output devices: Monitors	•	○	•	○	•	•
	Traditional CRT monitors	•	○	•	○	•	•
	Flat panel monitors (TFT)	•	○		○	•	○
	Liquid crystal displays (LCDs)	•	○	•	○	•	○
6	Output devices: Printers and plotters	•	○	•	•	•	•
	Laser printer	•	○	•	•	•	•
	Ink-jet printer	•	○	•	•	•	•
	Dot-matrix printer	•	○	•	•	•	
	Plotters	•		•	•	•	
7	Output devices: Others	•	•	•	•	•	
	Speakers	•	•	•	•	•	
	Control applications	•	•	•	•	•	•
	Actuators	•	•	•	•	•	
8	Back-up storage	•	•	•	•	•	•
	Hard disks	•	•	•	•	•	•
	USB memory stick	•	•		○		
	Disk access time		•		•	•	○
	Compact disc (CD)	•	•	•	•	•	•
	DVD	•	•		•	•	○
	Magnetic tape	•	•	•	•	•	•
9	The processor and memory	•	•	•	•	•	•
	Cental processing unit (CPU)	•		•	•	•	○
	Binary digits		•	•		•	
	Random access memory (RAM)	•	•	•	•	•	•
	Read only memory (ROM)	•	•	•	•	•	•

Page	Topic						
11 – 13	Databases	•	•	•	•	•	•
	Types of database	•	•				•
	Database fields	•	•	•	•	•	○
	Database records	•	•	•	•	•	○
	Searching and sorting databases	•	•	•	•	•	•
	Database reports	•	•	•	•	•	•
	Macros		•				
14, 15	Word processing	•	•	•	•	•	•
	Formatting	•	•	•	•	•	•
	Page design	•	•		•	•	•
	Style sheets		•		•	•	•
	Mailmerge	•		•	•	•	•
	Editing	•	•	•	•	•	•
	Spell-check		•	•	•	•	•
	Grammar check		•		•	•	
	Thesaurus					•	
16	Desktop publishing	•	•	•	•	•	•
	Formatting	•	•	•	•	•	•
	Text wrapping	•	•	•	•	•	○
	Layering	•		•	•	•	
	Graphic manipulation	•		•	•	•	•
17	Computer art and design	•	•	•	•	•	•
	Painting	•	•	•	•	•	○
	Drawing	•	•	•	•	•	○
	Computer aided design (CAD)			•	•	•	○
18	Presentation software		•		•	•	
	Slides		•		•	•	○
	Animation		•		•	•	○
19	Web site design and publishing	•	•				•
	Creating Web pages	•	•		•		
	Web site design	•	•			•	•
20	Spreadsheets	•	•	•	•	•	•
	Cells	•	•	•	•	•	•
	Calculations	•	•	•	•	•	○
	Formulae and functions	•	•	•	•	•	•
	Graphs and charts	•	•	•	•	•	•
21	Modelling and simulation	•	•	•	•	•	•
	Modelling packages	•	•	•	•	•	•
	Simulation packages	•	•	•			•
22	Data logging	•	•	•	•	•	•
	Sensors	•	•	•	•	•	•
	Analogue to digital				•		•
	Calibration	•					
23	Computer control	•	•	•	•	•	•
	Actuators	•	•		•	•	
	Feedback	•	•		•	•	
	Control examples	•	•	•	•	•	•
24	Programming languages	•	•	•	•		
	Algorithm	•	•	•	•		
	Variables	•			•		
	Programming techniques				•		
	Program flow charts		•	•			
25, 26	Operating systems	•	•	•	•	•	•
	Methods of operation	•	•	•	•	•	•
	Batch processing	•	•	•	•	•	•
	Real-time processing	•	•	•	•	•	
	Operating system tasks	•			•		
	Human–computer interface	•	•	•	•	•	
	Graphical user interface (GUI)	•	•	•	•	•	•
	Command line interface	•		•	•	•	
27, 28	Software development	•	•	•	•	•	
	System life cycle	•	•	•	•	•	
	Feasibility study	•	•	•	•	•	
	Top-down design	•	•				
	Data flow diagrams		•	•			
30, 31	Data	•	•	•	•	•	•
	Data representation (ASCII code)	•	•	•	•	•	
	Fixed length records	•		•	•	•	
	Variable length records	•			•	•	
	Calculating data size	•	•	•	•	•	
	Information and data	•	•			•	•
	Coding data	•	•	•	•	•	

Page	Topic						
32	Capturing and presenting data	•	•	•	•	•	•
	Range of input devices	•	•		•	•	•
	Turnaround documents				•		
	Questionnaires	•	•	•	•	•	•
	Presenting data	•	•	•	•	•	•
33	Verification and validation	•	•	•	•	•	•
	Verification	•	•	•	•	•	•
	Validation	•	•	•	•	•	•
	Presence check	•				•	•
	Character count			•			
	Range check	•	•	•	•	•	•
	Picture check	•	•	•	•	•	
	Table lookup		•		•		•
	Hash totals (control total)					•	
	Check digit	•	•	•	•	•	•
34	File handling	•	•	•		•	•
	Files (master, transaction, updating)	•		•		•	•
	System flow charts	•	•				
	File generations (grandfather, father, son)	•		•			
35	Security of data	•	•	•	•	•	•
	Care of disks	•	•			•	
	Back-ups	•	•	•	•	•	•
	Passwords	•	•	•	•	•	•
	Hackers	•	•	•	•	•	•
	Computer fraud		•		•		
	Viruses		•		•	•	•
37	Computer networks	•	•	•	•	•	•
	Local area networks (LAN)	•	•	•	•	•	•
	Wide area networks (WAN)	•	•	•	•	•	•
	Network topology (start, bus, ring)	•	•	•	•	•	
38	Network connections	•	•	•	•	•	•
	Cables			•	•	•	○
	Microwave				•	•	○
	Satellite			•	•	•	○
	Modem	•	•	•	•		•
	ADSL						•
	Network cards		•	•		•	○
39, 40	The Internet	•	•	•	•	•	•
	How to connect			•		•	○
	Internet service providers (ISPs)		•	•		•	•
	World Wide Web	•	•	•	•	•	•
	Web browsers	•	•	•	•	•	•
	General use of the Internet	•	•	•	•	•	•
	e-business/e-commerce		•	•	•	•	
	Web site design		•			•	•
	Researching information		•	•	•	•	•
41, 42	Communications and email	•	•	•	•	•	•
	Methods of communication	•	•	•	•	•	•
	Email	•	•	•	•	•	•
	Mobile phones	•	•	•	•	•	•
	Video conferencing			•	•	•	•
44 – 51	ICT in society	•	•	•	•	•	•
	Social, economic, ethical and moral effects	•	•	•	•	•	•
	Effect on jobs	•	•	•	•	•	•
52	Computers and the law	•	•	○	•	•	•
	The Data Protection Act, 1998	•	•	○	•	•	•
	The Computer Misuse Act, 1990	•	•	○	•	•	•
	The Copyright, Designs and Patents Act, 1998	•	•		•	•	•
53	Health and safety	•	•	•	•	•	•
	RSI and WRULD	•			•	•	•